Ted

I hope you enjoy my book

If You Try To Please Everybody, You Will Lose Your Ass

Jokes and Reflections on Business and Life

By
Stephen Einhorn

seinhorn@einhornassociates.com
www.ifyoutrytopleaseeverybody.com

Publisher: Stephen Einhorn, Milwaukee, Wisconsin
Cover Design: Jonathan Carnehl
Book Layout and Design: Alex Herrera
Sales & Marketing: Deeter, Strategic Public Relations
Favorite Baseball Team: Milwaukee Brewers
Favorite Restaurant: Heinemann's

Printed and bound by Worzalla Publishing, Stevens Point, Wisconsin

ISBN 978-0-615-19471-4

Dedication

The final chapter of this book is about success. This dedication is made to those who have contributed the most to whatever success I have had.

First, to my wife, Nancy, who has made me a better person. She knows what is right, expresses it crisply, practices it and is the joy of my life.

Next, to my sons, David and Daniel, who have grown into adults that make me proud to be their father. They are modest about their achievements, well liked and respected by those they meet. Both have followed my example and made fine choices in their mates, Cheryl and Terése, who are supportive and give them happiness. And currently, whatever success I have is enhanced by the presence of 5 terrific grandchildren, Rachel, Naomi, Mitchell, Emma and Henry.

No dedication would be complete without mentioning my mom, Rosalind, who provided me with the unsurpassed persistence necessary to accomplish anything difficult.

And finally, to my late father, Ben Einhorn (1915-2007), who set the example for me on how and why humor is so important.

Dad's last conversation with me went like this:

I said, "Dad, I understand that you will be in the hospital for 2 days --- and 2 days is too long."

"Steve" he said, "One-half hour in the hospital is too long."

Contents

Introduction

Twenty-five years ago, when I wrote the first edition of this book, I selected a group of jokes and stories that I found not only enjoyable but also clarified many things that I have learned about business and life. As you know, most successes in life relate to understanding yourself and getting along with others. This book contains much of what I have learned in these respects.

I am confident that you, as the reader of this book, will have your own thoughts as to whether these jokes, stories or comments have value or whether you have wasted your time and energy by reading them. If you are not satisfied with what you find, you have only yourself to blame for taking your limited time to read it; or, if you are a family member or friend, you have probably received your copy for free and have no justification whatsoever.

It is my hope that you do not make an effort to read this book in one sitting, but rather read one page at a time and think about it. It has been written with much of what I have learned over 65 years and I would recommend that you spend a few moments to consider each of these thoughts. My friends have told me that the bathroom is the best place to read this book.

They say that good advice is expensive. But, if you don't care for the advice, remember that a good joke or story has real value.*

Some of the most boring sentences I have ever read explain why jokes are funny. For me, the jokes and stories included here are fun and important because they have either taught me to re-examine my thinking or they clarified an aspect of life itself.

My hope is that this book will be read by young adults who have escaped from the politically correct content of the courses being taught at most American universities and want to have some fun and absorb a dose of business and adult life. You are the future and, in many respects, the ones for whom I have written this book.

---

* My niece, Hayley, told me this rabbinical story:
The prophet Elijah came down from heaven and met with the chief rabbi, and together they went into town to identify the person most likely to go to heaven. First, they spotted a very religious man, and the rabbi suggested that that person would be the first to go to heaven. But Elijah said, "No!" Then they came upon a very wealthy man who had given much to charity and the rabbi asked if this person would go to heaven first, and Elijah said, "No." Finally they came to a group of people who were laughing, and Elijah went up to the speaker and asked what he was doing. He said that he was a jester and that he told stories and jokes to make people laugh. Elijah said that he would be the first to go to heaven.

An old man and his grandson were traveling to Jerusalem with their donkey. When they started the journey, the old man sat on the donkey while his grandson walked ahead and guided the trip.

A passerby saw the scene and said, "You are a strong man. How can you let the little boy walk?"

The old man got off the donkey and the young boy climbed on top. When they reached Bethel, another passerby said to the old man, "You are an old man. The donkey is very strong. Why don't you both get on the donkey and ride?" And so they changed again.

As they approached Jerusalem they passed another stranger who commented, "Look at that poor donkey. You should be ashamed of yourselves. You have such a short way to go. Why don't you both walk and give the donkey a chance to rest?"

So, they got off the donkey and the donkey ran away.*

What is the moral of this story?

If you try to please everybody, you will lose your ass.

* From my former partner, the late Orville Mertz

Illustration by Jia Le Zhang

If you try to please everybody, you will lose your ass.

Good communications are the cornerstone of good business. If I consider myself to be an expert on communications, it is primarily because during my business career I have made virtually every error that the following jokes address.

The best communicators are the best listeners. In my family I was the slowest talker, so I had more opportunities than the others to listen. My mom was quite effective in her communications because she would repeat her ideas until the other person agreed. My Aunt Florence explained to me why I was so often interrupted when I spoke. "Stephen," she said, "in our family if you know what the other person is going to say, you are allowed to interrupt them." With this background you can understand how I had many opportunities to listen. In business, where successful communications result in successful business, listening well is its own reward.

If you believe that someone is talking at you and continues to speak without giving you a chance, you can always interrupt and say, "When you are through I have something I would like to say." At this point, I have found that the other person tends to stop speaking immediately and you get your chance to comment.

If you feel that you already have a great deal of experience in communications, that you listen well, that you plan ahead and always do your homework carefully, that you don't take yourself too seriously, that you show respect for others, that you provide clear and accurate answers, that you allow for different interpretations and reactions to common English, that you avoid sarcasm, that you have the ability to make complex issues simple; then I recommend that you skip this chapter and proceed immediately to the following chapter on arrogance.

Three 9-year-old girls were talking about their mothers.

The first said, "My mom is a consultant. She started a company 10 years ago and she has developed it into a very successful business."

The second said, "My mother is vice-president of a major biotech company. She flies around the world. She is responsible for 500 sales people and $500 million in revenue."

The last said, "My mom gives me as many hugs as I want."

Then, the first two exclaimed, "Lucky you!" *

To Improve Your Wealth --- Improve Your Hugging

Recently I went to a wedding and the bride's father pointed out that for a close relationship to work out it was only necessary to remember three phrases of three words each: (1) "I was wrong"; (2) "You are right"; and (3) "I love you." **

I have been a consultant and businessman for many years and it has taken me perhaps too long to learn that hugs are really important. To be successful we must learn how and when to give our customers, our staff, and our associates hugs (usually in the form of praise or support). And, to be really successful, we must learn how to give our family all the hugs they want.

---

* Thanks to Dr. Martha Welch.
** Thanks to Gene Levshetz.

Illustration by Pacharaporn Bamrungphong

My mom gives me as many hugs as I want.

On the first day at a Catholic private school a new student in the lunch line noticed a basket of apples with a sign that said, "Take only one apple. God is watching."

He continued to the end of the food line where he saw a tray of cookies, and he decided to put a sign on it.

After lunch his teacher, Sr. Mary, addressed the class and expressed annoyance that all of the cookies had been eaten. Sr. Mary asked the sign writer to come to the front of the class and read the sign aloud.

The new student went to the front of the class and read the sign. It said, "Take as many cookies as you want. God is watching the apples."

Give Accurate Directions and God Will Watch the Cookies

Since what is clear to you is not necessarily clear to others, the quality of your directions will determine their consequences. When you give directions, make sure they are complete and ask for confirmation that the recipient understands them as you intended. In other words, if you want to improve the chances that your directions will be followed, either ask the other person to state in his words what he believes are your instructions or put a sign on the cookies to clarify that God is also watching the cookies.

Illustration by Ryan Carter

God is watching the apples.

An old man in a nursing home asked an old woman to guess his age. When she asked him, "Why should I tell you?" he replied, "Just to see if you can!"

She thought about it for a minute and then said to him, "Okay, I'll tell you if you take off your pants."

He did and she immediately started to feel his private parts. After 5 minutes she said, "You are 92."

He said, "That is right, but how did you know?"

She said, "You told me yesterday."

Be Considerate --- Remember That the Older We Get, The More We Forget

To paraphrase Mark Twain, "People who are older can't remember anything (whether it happened or not)." In dealing with older people, speak slowly, be especially clear and give them extra time to process information. Decision-making can be more difficult for older folks and fundamental financial decisions are particularly tough. Seek their active participation and response to issues and provide a written copy of your recommendations. This will reduce the likelihood of future misunderstandings and provide a solid basis for agreement. This is the best process I know for making a lasting impression with the aged without having to take your pants down.

Have you heard about the latest quiz show idea? It's not like the original quiz shows where they gave you a question and you had to provide the answer. It's not like the newer quiz shows where they gave you an answer and you had to devise the question. In this brand new quiz, they give you the answer and they give you the question --- and you have to guess who submitted the information.

If A Question Seems A Bit Saucy --- Consider The Source

When answering a customer's question, your goal is to strike the proper balance between satisfying the customer through clear and precise answers and protecting your firm's interests. Customers who are seriously interested in your products or services want to be sure they are making the right decision, and they may tend to ask what appears to be an excessive number of questions. When this happens, it is common to become irritated or impatient and feel that your time is being wasted. Yet it is usually best to give the customer the benefit of the doubt because answering questions graciously, even "excessive" questions, improves a customer's confidence level.

When the customer is through, it should be your turn to ask questions, and you should concentrate on learning what obstacles stand between you and success.

Sometimes, excessive questions are a sign of disinterest, or worse. They may be seeking confidential information that they are not entitled to or information that they could use to your detriment. When this occurs it is time for you to ask yourself, who is asking the question and why are they asking it? If the question doesn't feel right to you, there is a reason that you may not be able to identify at the moment. When that happens, don't answer the question.

From a court transcript ---
> Q: Are you sexually active?
> A: No. I just lie there.

Accurate Answers Require Active Thinking --- Don't Just Lie There

There is a big distinction between accurate answers and technically correct answers: It is usually better to be accurate and if the answer is "Yes," just say "Yes." This is true, even if the technically correct answer is to say that you just lie there.

A man walked into a bar in a town strange to him. He noticed in the corner two young women. He approached them and they had a drink. After the drink he asked them if they would like to have some fun. They agreed and went to a nearby bedroom. He asked them if it would be all right for both of them to make love to him. They said that it would be OK, but he should realize that while he had sex with the first one the other would play the flute and when he made love to the second, the other would play the cello. They then proceeded to have wonderful sex together.

The next day the man went into the same bar. One woman looked at the other and asked, "Do you think he will remember us?"

They May Forget Your Name --- But They Will Probably Remember What You Did

It is not the similarities but the differences between people that make life so interesting. An ordinary experience for you may be an exceptional one for me. This presents a common challenge to our communication skills: How does one distinguish what someone already knows (and doesn't want to hear again) from what someone doesn't know and would benefit from hearing? Of course, in some cases one can be certain to remember: for example, who played the flute and who played the cello.

A man and a large dog walked by as a new neighbor walked outside for the first time. The newcomer asked the man, "Does your dog bite?"

"No" was the reply. So the new neighbor petted the dog and the dog immediately bit the new neighbor.

The bitten man yelled, "I thought you said that your dog doesn't bite."

The man replied, "I did say that, but this isn't my dog."

Ask The Right Question --- Or You May Get Bitten By The Wrong Dog

Think carefully before asking a question so that you ask the right question. By taking your time and continuing to think about your goals, you will improve your ability to ask the right questions. Remember that if you ask the wrong question, you are likely to get the wrong answer, and the results may bite you.

Illustration by Kelly Grabko

Good thing your dog doesn't bite.

A family was eating dinner when their youngest child asked his mother, "Are dead flies good to eat?"

"No!" said the mother. "What makes you ask such a ridiculous question?"

"You had one in your salad. But it is gone now."

Don't Criticize Their Question --- And You Will Not Have To Eat Any Dead Flies

If you don't give respect to the questions of others, you won't learn what you should know --- or help others learn what they think they have a need to know. So, be patient and give their questions the attention they require. That way, you will allow them to get all of the dead flies on the table.

The husband went hunting, shot a deer and came home with it. His wife cooked the deer and served it for dinner. She asked her son what he thought he was eating.

The son guessed:

"Pork?" The answer was "No."
"Beef?" The answer was "No."
"Lamb?" The answer was "No."
Finally, her son gave up.

Mom said, "Let me give you a hint. It is what I call your father all the time."
"Oh, my God," said the son. "We are eating asshole."

If Your Question Is Not Clear --- The Answer Won't Be Dear

When you are doing something for the first time, it can be disruptive to others. We all need guidance to adjust to change and we all want to feel comfortable. Here are some thoughts:

(1) When you are presenting something that is new, don't overwhelm others with too many or too few * choices;

(2) Give them a solid basis and justification for the change; and, above all

(3) Don't ask them to guess deer when there are other more interesting, but less desirable alternatives.

---

* Like the secretary who filed everything in two files and labeled them "Miscellaneous" and "Other than Miscellaneous."

A father greeted his wife at the hospital after first seeing their new baby boy. This was the fourth boy in their family, and the first one who didn't have red hair and green eyes. The father said, "Shaun has blue eyes and blond hair. He doesn't look like our other three children.   Are you sure he is my child?"

"Yes," said his wife.

Many years went by, and each year the husband asked his wife to verify that Shaun was indeed his child.

Finally, the couple became old; the wife was on her deathbed. The husband asked one more time, "Is Shaun my child?"

"Yes," said his wife, "but I don't want to mislead you any longer. The other three are not!"

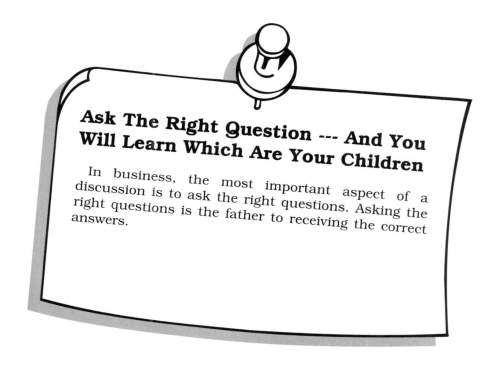

Ask The Right Question --- And You Will Learn Which Are Your Children

In business, the most important aspect of a discussion is to ask the right questions. Asking the right questions is the father to receiving the correct answers.

Illustration by Audre Delany

The other three are not.

A company with 400 employees decided to provide a new pension plan for its employees. The plan could only go into effect if all 400 employees signed on. All but one, a shipping foreman, had agreed to join, and the day before the deadline all of his co-workers tried to convince him to sign on.

On deadline day, when the president of the company was alerted to the problem, he invited the shipping foreman to his office on the 10th floor of the factory. He opened the window to his office and told the shipping foreman that every living employee must sign on for the new pension plan, and, if the shipping foreman didn't sign, he would have to jump out the window.

The shipping foreman signed immediately. The president asked him why he had changed his mind so rapidly. The foreman replied, "No one ever explained it to me clearly before."

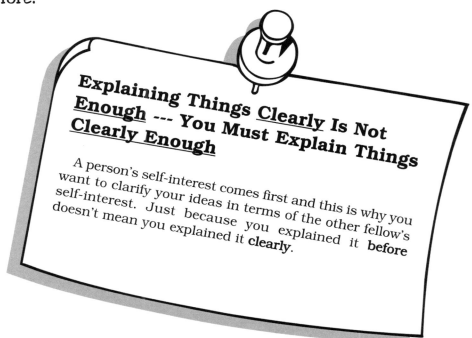

Explaining Things <u>Clearly</u> Is Not Enough --- You Must Explain Things <u>Clearly Enough</u>

A person's self-interest comes first and this is why you want to clarify your ideas in terms of the other fellow's self-interest. Just because you explained it **before** doesn't mean you explained it **clearly**.

Two prostitutes were walking down the street in Alabama, and opposite them came two nuns in their black habits.

The younger prostitute asked her friend, "Honey, what are those two?"

"Those are nuns," said her friend.

"And what are nuns?" questioned the younger.

"Nuns, honey, ain't had none. They ain't gettin' none. And they ain't gonna get none."

If You Want Something Badly, Do It Yourself --- Or You Ain't Gonna Get None

If it is truly important to learn something, find out for yourself. Get as close to the source of information as possible. No one is micromanaging when he delves into details on important matters. Business information, even when neatly typed, is often inaccurate. Bad information generates bad decisions, and, if you make too many bad decisions, when it comes time to collect your paycheck, you ain't gonna get none.

A company owner was concerned that one of his factories was inefficient, so he called an efficiency expert. The efficiency expert went to the factory and observed an employee next to his machine.

The worker was doing no work, and the efficiency expert asked, "What are you doing?"

The worker answered, "Nothing."

Then the efficiency expert approached a second worker who also was doing no work. He asked again, "What are you doing?" Once again the reply was "Nothing."

With a gleam in his eyes, the expert approached the owner and announced, "You, sir, have a problem! Duplication!"

Almost All Serious Business Problems Are Merely Repetitions Of A Single Problem

At work, when you discover a problem, it is rare for that problem to have occurred for the first time. When you delve into the matter you will probably find that it is endemic to your company.

So, when you check out a problem, find out what the company has done in similar situations. Then, work with your team to confirm what the problem is so that you can rectify it. This process is usually quite challenging.   Just remember that one man's "inefficiency" is another man's " duplication."

A couple of high school girls who were quite fashion conscious were discussing how atoms lose and gain electrons to form ions, yet still remain the same element. One of the students explained, "It's like you change your outfits, but your personality stays the same."

To Simplify A Complex Problem --- Put The Idea In The Other Fellow's Terms

Virtually all complex concepts can be explained simply. Many people have the ability to take simple concepts and make them complex. If you are going to be successful, you must learn to clarify and make the complex simple. Try to explain things in terms of the other person's understanding of the world. Change your outfit, but keep your personality.

A little girl said to her mother, "I would like some ice cream."

The mother said to the girl, "What else do you say."

The little girl replied, "Now."

If You Really Want Ice Cream --- Say "Please"

"Bring up a child in the way she should grow and when she grows up she shall not depart from it" is how the proverb goes. The problem in teaching, whether it is a child or a business associate, is that circumstances themselves determine whether it is better to seek a result through questions or through directives. Often it is just more effective to provide specific instructions like "You must say 'please.'"

Illustration by Katie Gamb

Now!

It was time to go to sleep and I asked my son, Danny, to put away his video game. An hour later he was still playing the game. Sarcastically, I said to him, "Dan, you did a nice job putting away the video game!"

He replied, "You did a nice job telling me."

Remember That Sarcasm Is An Effective Tool Only With Those Who Agree With You

Sarcasm is usually not an effective way to negotiate because it is a two-edged sword that too frequently leads to animosity. The problem is that sarcasm leaves a deep imprint on those who don't appreciate it and has a lasting negative effect on those who don't agree with you. In these cases, the short-term satisfaction you receive from your cleverness usually does not justify the long-term deterioration of your relationship.

On the other hand, I have found that sarcasm can be extremely effective when working with someone who agrees with you because it can crystallize the issue at hand, provide a needed source of humor, and furnish the teller with a unique form of satisfaction. This is especially effective when dealing with your father.

Correction

..........from the NY Times in early 2003...

"The New York Times made a long, valiant effort to report Chemical Bank's earnings the week before last, but for every step forward toward precision, it seemed to slip two steps back. First came an error in a brief earnings report, followed the next day with a correction. But that correction somehow managed to address only part of the error, and the proper correction appeared the following day, surely ending the matter. But it was not to be. So, in what The Times sincerely hopes is the last word on the subject, here is what Chemical earned ....."

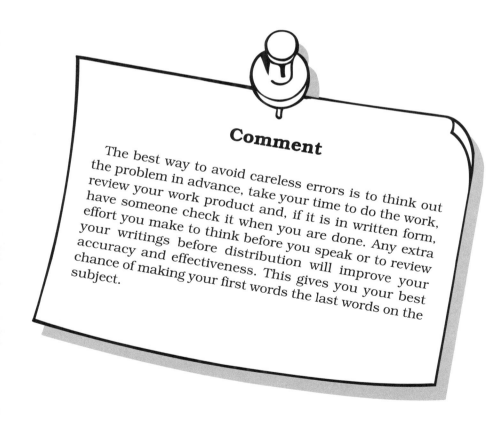

Comment

The best way to avoid careless errors is to think out the problem in advance, take your time to do the work, review your work product and, if it is in written form, have someone check it when you are done. Any extra effort you make to think before you speak or to review your writings before distribution will improve your accuracy and effectiveness. This gives you your best chance of making your first words the last words on the subject.

A wife complained that her husband was obsessed with sex. After several years she was able to convince him to go to a psychiatrist to discuss his sexual appetite. The psychiatrist advised the patient that he was going to address the problem by drawing pictures and asking questions. He drew a few lines with a pencil and asked the patient what he saw.

The patient replied, "I see two people having sex."

The psychiatrist took a bold pen, drew a completely different picture and asked the fellow what he saw.

The patient replied, "I see two people having sex."

Next, the psychiatrist took out a bottle of ink and poured it on the page and asked again what the fellow saw.

The patient replied, "I see two people having sex."

The psychiatrist said, "You have a serious sex problem. You are probably a sex pervert."

The patient replied, "No, I'm not! You keep drawing sexy pictures." *

No Matter How Clear Your Picture Is --- He Still May Be Thinking Of Sex

People hear what they want to hear, feel what they want to feel, and see what they want to see. So, if sexy pictures are what they want to see, they will see sexy pictures.

---

*My dad told me this when he was 91.

Illustration by Katie M^C Donnell

You keep drawing sexy pictures.

Jeffrey was planning to rob a bank after he read a newspaper article about a successful bank robbery. He decided to follow the example of the successful bank robber, so he went to the bank, took out his gun and demanded, "I want an undetermined amount of cash."

If You Are Not Clear In Your Fees --- You Will Not Collect With Ease

When you are negotiating for the price of your goods or the fees for your services, there must be a clear-cut understanding of your value-added and the compensation you will receive for it. This must be presented succinctly and agreed upon by both sides. State the fee at the beginning, and make sure the other party agrees with it. This way, when the deal is done, you won't end up with an undetermined amount of cash.

A mother and her daughter went to a department store at Christmas time. The daughter saw Santa Claus in the distance, ran up to him, and received a warm greeting.

Santa asked, "And what would you like for Christmas?"

The little girl became upset and complained, "Didn't you get my e-mail?"

For Important E-mails --- Follow Up And Call To Make Sure They Were Received

One major problem with the e-mails you send is that the recipient probably receives so many that yours will likely get less attention than you want. If your e-mail is not important (like e-mailing one of these jokes) then it probably doesn't matter. But, if you care about the e-mail and it requires an immediate response, confirm receipt by calling after you send it. So, phone Santa if your e-mail is important. Otherwise, he probably won't know what you want for Christmas.

After a big race, two horses were talking. The first horse said, "You certainly ran a terrific race today. What got into you?"

The other horse replied, "My owner told me that if I ran a good race today, I could have an extra bale of hay. And that ain't money!"

Be Flexible --- Some Horses Like Hay; Some Like Money

It is your responsibility to figure out what the other guy wants. He might want hay or he might want money.

Illustration by Ashley Webster

Some horses like hay; some like money.

A man walking down the street was approached by a stranger. The stranger said to him, "Is it true that you were in Las Vegas last October 4, and that you met a Mrs. Jones there and had an affair?"

"Yes," said the man, "That is all true."

The stranger glared at him and said, "Well, I have a surprise for you! I am her husband, Mr. Jones, and it is not my pleasure to tell you that I did not like your affair at all."

"Well," said the man. "The affair was not a pleasure and I did not enjoy it at all, either."

Just Because They Should Be Satisfied --- Doesn't Mean They Will Be Satisfied

What makes English so much fun is that identical words spoken with various intonations by different people have different meanings. From small distinctions do large disagreements spring.

Our firm is in Milwaukee and my assistant had the job of obtaining some information from a prominent Japanese bank in New York. After talking to several people and unsuccessfully explaining who she was, she was finally connected to a very courteous Japanese gentleman.

"Hello, this is Jacky from Einhorn Associates."

"Oh? Who?"

"Jacky, from Einhorn Associates."

"Who?"

"Einhorn Associates."

"Where?"

"Milwaukee!"

"Ah, Milwaukee, she off today!"

All People Speak Their Own Language --- And They Understand <u>Only</u> What They Mean

Of course, you all know that Milwaukee is a place, and not a person, located somewhere in Minnesota. Admittedly, those folks who live in Wisconsin would claim that Milwaukee was in Wisconsin.

In selling, there is a lot of confusion and, in particular, there are two types of "yeses": "Yes, I understand" and "Yes, I agree." Confusing these two meanings of yes are the basis for many business misunderstandings. Japanese and Chinese folk in particular use "yes" to mean they understand --- so be sure you also understand.

Several years ago in a prison there was only one book, a joke book. All of the inmates read the joke book and after a couple of years, each had memorized the book. Since there was one joke on each page, they started to take shortcuts, and before long the first joke was called Joke Number 1, and the second, Joke Number 2, and so on.

When an inmate wanted to tell a joke, he would just say, "Joke Number 6" and everyone would laugh.

Along came a new inmate. He read the joke book, memorized each joke by number, and during breakfast yelled out, "Joke Number 2." No one laughed.

He repeated, "Joke Number 2." Once again, no one laughed.

Later he asked one of the other inmates, "Why didn't anyone laugh? Number 2 is the funniest joke!"

"Some people just can't tell a joke," the other inmate explained.

You Can Be Successful --- Even If You Can't Tell A Joke

As a salesperson, it is your responsibility to adapt to other people. It is up to you to get your message across in a way that will make them feel comfortable and satisfied. This will assure your success even if you can't tell a joke.

Illustration by Marie Risa Johnson

Some people just can't tell a joke.

A Floridian read in the paper that he could take a trip to the Bahamas for $2.50. He went to the travel office, paid his $2.50, and asked for the Bahamas trip.

At the pier he was knocked unconscious by a man with a club, and when he awoke, he found that he was rowing his way, along with a dozen others, from Florida to the Bahamas.

He looked at the man next to him and found out that this unfortunate fellow had also been hit with a club. He turned to the fellow and said, "My Lord, this is terrible! After we arrive in the Bahamas, I hope they fly us back to Miami!"

The fellow looked at him and said, "They didn't last year!"*

Learn From Experience --- Find Out What They Did Last Year

Learn whatever you can about your customer's background, experience and prejudices. Otherwise, you will make the same mistakes others made last year.

---

*Thanks to Joel Sandberg, my brother-in-law.

I was in the Copenhagen airport waiting for my plane to Frankfurt to depart. In the waiting room next to me was an old man who asked me if I could watch his carry-on luggage for a few minutes.

I asked him, "Are you going to Frankfurt?"

"No," he said. "I am going to the men's room."

If You Answer A Question With A Question --- You Probably Won't Get A Good Answer

Possibly you are thinking that this is an example of me not asking a more precise question rather than the vague, "Are you going to Frankfurt?" I think that would be a valid comment.

But, I would like to tackle this discussion differently. I acknowledge that the better answer to the question of whether I would watch this man's luggage was either "Yes" or "No." And when I answered his question with a question, I deserved the resulting confusion.

Answering a question with a question is almost always a bad practice because it does not respect the original questioner and, in effect, what I did by asking, "Are you going to Frankfurt" is to take control.

So, don't take control by asking more questions: Just say "yes" and watch their luggage.

An Irishman walked into a bar and told the bartender, "I want to show you the most amazing thing in the world!"

The bartender watched while the customer opened a small brief case and took out a miniature piano. A small man, around 1-foot tall, also hopped out of the briefcase and started to play the piano magnificently.

"Where did you find this little fellow?" asked the bartender.

"Last year I went to Ireland, and while I was meandering through the countryside, I came upon a leprechaun. The leprechaun told me that I was the first person he had seen in 1,000 years, and as such, I was entitled to one wish. I thought for a minute, and then I made my wish."

At this point the bartender interrupted, "You mean to tell me that you had one wish, and you wished for a 1-foot pianist?"

"Not exactly," replied the patron. "The leprechaun was a bit hard of hearing. Actually, I asked for a 12-inch penis."

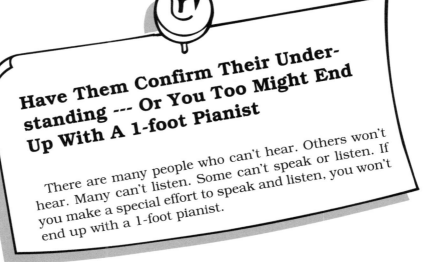

Have Them Confirm Their Understanding --- Or You Too Might End Up With A 1-foot Pianist

There are many people who can't hear. Others won't hear. Many can't listen. Some can't speak or listen. If you make a special effort to speak and listen, you won't end up with a 1-foot pianist.

The discussion at a party centered on the effects of a pregnant mother's actions on her unborn child. There was a woman who did not believe that pre-natal activities would affect a baby's life, and she argued, "Take my mother, for instance. During her pregnancy, she was hit on the head with a phonograph record and it didn't do me any harm --- any harm --- any harm ---." *

If They Repeat Themselves --- Listen, Listen, Listen

Many of your customers had parents who one would think were hit over the head with phonograph records while they were in a pre-natal state. This is why they keep repeating themselves. Your job is to listen --- listen --- listen. Eventually, your turn to talk will come and your patience will not have done you any harm --- any harm --- any harm.

---

* If you are under 50, ask your father or mother to explain this joke.

The substitute teacher thought she had done particularly well with one class when she received a card from one of the students. She opened the card, and it read, "Thanks! In such a short time you taught us everything you know."

Recognize That They May Think They Know Everything --- Or At Least Everything You Know

What do you say when someone thinks he is following your advice but has only understood a fraction of what you said or meant? Most of the time, it is best simply to apologize and try again, because people don't like to be told they did not understand.

In serious distressful situations, when things become tense and personal, acknowledge that this is the case, and say something like, "It hurts me that you..." This is often effective because usually others don't want to hurt you even if they know everything.

Having been warned not to divulge that she was a widow living alone, a woman tried to persuade a persistent telemarketer that she did not need a cemetery plot. The salesman, after extended efforts, became frustrated and said, "If I could just speak to your husband, I'm sure I could sell him one."

"I don't think so," replied the widow, "He is using his right now!"

In Business Don't Expect Perfect Confidentiality --- Unless They Are In A Cemetery Plot

Many times in business, what is to be kept confidential is a matter of judgment. If you discover corporate theft, a serious misuse of corporate property, major customer dissatisfaction, or serious conduct violations, they should not be kept confidential and you should abide by your responsibility to alert your employer.

On the other hand, things that might hurt others without any corresponding benefit; corporate know-how that is unique and provides your firm with a competitive advantage, and information that others have no need to know should be kept confidential. In particular, written confidentiality statements are to be followed. If you sign a confidentiality statement and violate it, you may end up wishing that you were in a cemetery plot.

A young boy was visiting his friend's house and noticed that there was no clock in his friend's room. "How come you don't have a clock in your room?" asked the boy. The answer came, "Why do I need a clock? I have a trumpet."

"A trumpet! What good is that?"

"When I want to know what time it is in the middle of the night, I go outside and blow my trumpet. My neighbor yells at me, 'Why are you playing the trumpet? Don't you know it's 3 o'clock in the morning?'

So what do I need a clock for?"

Listen Carefully --- His Trumpet May Trump Your Idea

If you don't have a really good idea, listen to the other guy's idea first. If you do have a really good idea, listen to the other guy's idea first. You might have a clock, but he might have a trumpet!

Illustration by Jodi Schomaker

What do I need a clock for?

Chapter 2
BEHAVIOR COUNTS

Too many times during my business career I have run into unacceptable behavior, and, though I hate to admit it, sometimes I have been the culprit. To my way of thinking, arrogance and excessive greed top the negative list, and respect and humility top the positive list of desirable business behaviors because these provide long-term benefits.

Arrogance is a most irritating trait because it magnifies disrespect, belittles the person who is subject to it, and too often is accompanied by excessive greed. Arrogance is often successful in the short run because it intimidates and catches us unprepared. My experience is that those who are most successful act with genuine humility, probably because they recognize that their receptionists know more than they about many aspects of their business. If you have been fortunate enough to have had an outstanding education, be especially careful to avoid even the appearance of arrogance. Remember that you are not a dawn unto your own day.

When confronted with arrogance, there are three strategies you might want to consider: (1) change or end the discussion and leave; (2) show a deference and humility in your own demeanor and hope that the tone of the conversation will change; or (3) state more positively and aggressively than you usually would your ideas and thoughts. Whatever you do, concentrate your responses on good reasoning and avoid emotional responses.

Humility requires us to value kindness, patience and graciousness, traits often lacking in our depersonalized, computer-driven society. So, when you are subjected to arrogance or greed, remember how Henny Youngman, the famous one-sentence-tells-all comedian, described himself. "Humility has made me a 100% better person."

A man went into the butcher shop and asked, "Do you have any brains?"

"Yes," replied the butcher. "We have Ph.D. brains for $50 a pound."

"Do you have any other brains?" asked the man.

"Yes, we have engineer brains for $250 a pound," said the butcher.

"Do you have any other brains?" the man asked.

"Yes, we have businessmen brains for $2,000 a pound."

"$2,000!" exclaimed the buyer. "Why so much?"

Said the butcher, "Do you know how many businessmen it takes to make a pound of brains?"

Recognize That Many Businessmen Believe That Their Brains Are Worth $2,000 Per Pound

Many entrepreneurs have started their own businesses, and they know more about them than anyone else. When they are successful, many think they know more about your business than you do. Also, though you may be a specialist in your business, many of your customers believe they know more about your product or service than you. In business, great brainpower is dependent upon experience. Businessmen who forget this will likely butcher their results.

Illustration by Brittany R. Miller

Do you know how many businessmen it takes to make a pound of brains?

A lion walked through the jungle and asked each animal in turn to name the King of the Jungle. The rabbit, the deer, the tall giraffe all responded, "Mr. Lion, you are King of the Jungle."

Then the lion came upon an elephant and asked the elephant to name the King of the Jungle. Without saying a word, the elephant picked up the lion, turned him around, and dropped him against the side of the mountain. The lion, dazed, struggled to his feet and staggered over to the elephant.

The lion then said, "Just because you don't know the answer doesn't mean you have to get so mad."

Maintain Your Humility --- And You Won't Tangle With An Elephant

I once had two partners who exuded arrogance. Their arrogance intimidated me and was often effective in obtaining their aims. But, arrogance only works for the short run, leaves a bad taste, and is ineffective for the long run. Of course, humility also helps in the short run if you meet up with an elephant.

Illustration by Lauren Rubin

I thought I was King of the Jungle.

Two statues, one of a man, the other of a woman, faced each other in Central Park. One day a genie came and touched the male statue and granted him one wish.

"Could you bring to life the woman statue that I have been looking at for 100 years?"

The genie brought the woman statue to life. The male statue immediately walked to the female statue and said to her, "Do you want to do it?"

"Yes," she replied.

"OK," he said, "You hold the pigeons and I'll poop on them."

All Actions Have Consequences ---
If You Are A Pigeon, Be Careful

Revenge, like jealousy, is among the worst of all faults. As Shakespeare wrote, "It (jealousy) doth mock the food it feeds on." However, there is a rhythm in life, and when we follow that rhythm we understand that all actions have consequences. So, if you are a pigeon, be careful where you poop.

Illustration by Lauren Rubin

Be careful where you poop.

A new golfer had just purchased a beautiful outfit and took her first golf lesson from the assistant pro. On the next day the head pro came to work, and met her for the first time.

He greeted her. "Welcome to the club. Do you want to learn to play golf, Ma'am?"

"No, thank you," she replied. "I learned to play yesterday."

Don't Try To Teach Your Customers What They Learned Yesterday

One of the two junior partners I mentioned earlier, perhaps the more aggressive one, once told me that only one out of ten of my ideas was a good one. Let me ignore the obvious disrespect and arrogance of the comment (or its possible accuracy) and suggest to you that when you run into this type of arrogance, don't ignore it, but rather think about the lady who learned to play golf yesterday. If you are the pro and they know it all, you probably don't want another chance to teach them tomorrow.

A stranger was seated next to little Donny, age 12, on the plane. The stranger turned to little Donny and said, "Let's talk. I've heard that flights go quicker if you strike up a conversation with your fellow passenger."

Donny, who had just opened his book, closed it slowly, and said to the stranger, "What would you like to discuss?"

"Oh, I don't know," said the stranger. "How about politics?"

"OK," said Donny. "That could be an interesting topic. But let me ask you a question first. A horse, a cow, and a deer all eat grass, the same stuff. Yet a deer excretes little pellets, while a cow turns out a flat patty, and a horse produces clumps of dried grass. Why do you suppose that is?"

"Gee whiz," said the stranger. "I have no idea."

"Well, then," said little Donny, "How is it that you feel qualified to discuss politics, when you don't know shit?"

Just Because You Are An Expert Doesn't Mean You Know Shit

It is best to be modest when you explain what you believe you know and receptive when others tell you what they think you don't know. Put forth your ideas without the appearance of being a "know-it-all" and speak respectfully, with a soft, clear voice in a confident, gracious manner. This maximizes your chances for success, even if you don't know shit.

Jack owned a bar. One day he visited his bar and noticed that when the bartender sold a $10 drink, he put $5 in the cash register and $5 in his pocket.

A few months passed and Jack returned to his bar. This time he noticed that when the bartender sold a $10 drink he put the whole $10 in his pocket.

Jack went up to the bartender and asked, "What happened? Aren't we partners anymore?"

Beware Of Partners Who Want The Entire $10

Where there are corporate profits to be divided, management often has trouble with the fine line between sharing and greed. Generosity is a wonderful thing, but greed is much easier to find and more realistic to expect. Human instinct guides people away from sharing, and this tendency increases when it can be accomplished without recourse.

Some managers want their shareholders to do well and will sacrifice their own rewards in bad years and share generously with their shareholders in good years. You should avoid those companies that proclaim interest in their shareholders but allocate compensation disproportionately in favor of management. Be especially concerned with those managers who claim they are sharing but take the entire $10.

Illustration by Daniel R. Willaims

Aren't we partners any more?

A successful executive was on his deathbed. His doctor had told him that he had only a few hours to live, and three of his closest associates gathered around him.

"This is a man of great patience," said the first friend.

"And a man of great wisdom," added the second.

The third completed the sentiments with, "And a man of great charity."

At this point, the dying man arose and said, "And what about my great modesty?"

Keep Your Outstanding Attributes To Yourself — Especially Your Modesty

My father helped to write my Bar Mitzvah speech and included the phrase, "Plant humility in my soul." Allow others to recognize your positive attributes and allow them to declare your modesty.

An actor, looking for a job, visited an agent. He walked into the agent's office, hopped on the desk, and started flying about the room. For five minutes, he looped and swung and dove through the air, while remaining aloft. Then he landed feet first on the ground, sat down in a chair, and looked at the agent.

The agent looked back and asked, "What else can you do besides imitate birds?"

True Appreciation Appears Only In The Dictionary --- What Else Can You Do Besides Imitate Birds?

My father warned me that gratitude is a word that appears only in the dictionary. Recognize and express appreciation to others for those actions that deserve it. On the other hand, don't assume anyone will appreciate the work you do --- even if you can imitate birds.

A disgruntled customer went to the return desk to complain about a dress she had purchased. She complained vociferously to the return service clerk. For five minutes she repeated her complaints and became increasingly shrill in her expression.

The return service clerk, after hearing more about her complaints than desired, said, "Madam, suppose we refund your money, send you another dress without charge, fire the salesperson, close the store, and have the manager shot. Would that be satisfactory?"

Show Genuine Sympathy --- But Don't Shoot The Manager

Limit your complaints to the important stuff, and think about the alternatives to complaining --- like saying nothing. Think of a kind way to discuss an issue or take the blame for a problem yourself. This will provide everyone around you with good feelings and in most cases the results will most certainly make you feel good.

It is easy to complain and some customers or employees have a real talent for making complaints. No matter how hard you try, there are instances when you cannot please them. So, just remember that emotion and neurosis are part of us all. Listen carefully, think out what is the real problem, and show sympathy. This will help overcome the problem and allow you to satisfy your customers without having to kill the manager.

A hospital patient was worried and thought that he had contracted pneumonia. He said, "Doctor, I've heard of cases where a doctor treated a patient for pneumonia, and he ended up dying of something else."

"Don't worry," said the doctor, "When I treat a patient for pneumonia, he dies of pneumonia."

Seek A Second Opinion --- And You Won't Die From Pneumonia

The doctor's answer here is a "know-it-all," arrogant answer. It is not supportive and doesn't contribute toward reassuring the patient. So, when you receive advice that adds to the problem, it is usually best to think about the situation yourself and to seek a second opinion from a knowledgeable, independent, friendly source. This will improve both your comfort level and the possibility that you have a reasonable answer and can better resolve your dilemma.

As the reader, you will probably agree that a better answer by the doctor might have been, "When I treat a patient for pneumonia, the patient is cured and doesn't die from either pneumonia or any other disease." But, that isn't funny, and this is supposed to be a joke book, so we will stick with "he dies of pneumonia."

At a major fund raising event, a man raised his hand and spoke, "My name is Harold Jones. We have a clothing store at 555 Delancy St. It is open from 9 to 6 on weekdays and 12 to 5 on Sundays. We give good value in our clothing and do excellent tailoring. I would like to pledge $10,000 anonymously."

Be Careful Of People Who Publicize Their Anonymity

Most people try to say what they mean. In negotiations it is frequently the case that there is a marked difference between what people say and what they mean. This can be intentional or unintentional. Success in negotiations will be determined by how well you decode these mixed messages. Ask yourself whether their behavior seems reasonable and, if not, ask them to justify their positions. Be especially careful of people who pledge $10,000 anonymously.

Two businessmen, Tom and Jim, discussed a problem over lunch. The discussion became heated and finally Tom took a large container of ketchup off the table and poured it all over Jim.

Ten seconds later Tom realized what a fool he had been and said, "I am really embarrassed that I doused you with ketchup."

Jim replied, "You should see a psychiatrist!" And Tom agreed.

Six months later, the two men met again and went out for lunch.

The conversation became heated and once again, Tom threw ketchup on his friend. "I thought you were going to see a psychiatrist," said Jim.

"I did."

"Well, it doesn't seem to have helped you."

Tom looked at his friend and said, "Seeing the psychiatrist helped a lot. Now I don't feel embarrassed."

There Is No Need To Feel Embarrased If You Throw A Little Ketchup

When you make a mistake, work at it and believe it is corrected, don't be surprised if it reappears. The best and most experienced entrepreneurs continually improve their solutions to complex problems. They often do it wrong the first time and continue their efforts until they figure out what really works. Don't be afraid that you are making the wrong decision when, after a reasonable amount of thought, you tentatively decide what to do. Go for it. Throw the ketchup and don't be embarrassed!

A young man hired by a supermarket reported for his first day of work. The manager greeted him with a warm handshake and a smile, gave him a broom and said, "Your first job will be to sweep out the store."

"But I'm a college graduate!" the young man replied indignantly.

"Oh, I'm sorry about the misunderstanding," said the manager. "Here, give me the broom. I'll show you how."

If You Are Highly Educated --- Keep It To Yourself

If you are highly educated, be careful not to act with arrogance, especially when you are with those who possess less education. Arrogance is easy to find, can often be intimidating and is almost always irritating. So, if someone wants to teach you something, let him. Accept the fact that to sweep properly takes experience, and it takes training to use a broom effectively.

Illustration by Jared Martin

I'll show you how.

Chapter 3
VALUE ADDED

Value is a complex concept with many meanings. We could probably agree that to be successful and provide value, we must help our customers achieve their dreams. Since others live by their own values, our chance to provide substantial value depends on how much we know about how they think, how they feel, what they want and how they dream.

The concept works both ways: When we receive a high-quality product or service, it will likely be expensive and yet a good value. For example, our firm occupies a high quality, expensive office that provides much value in terms of comfort for our staff and warmth for our clients.

Measuring value for clients is most often a qualitative and not a quantitative issue. Let me give you a few examples of how difficult it can be to get a quantitative measure for services rendered:

(1) When we work for a buyer, our goal is to help our client purchase a business at a low price. One time I met with a seller who said that he would accept $7 million for his business. After I told that price to our client (the buyer), our client asked the seller how much he wanted for the business. The seller told the buyer $8 million. The buyer paid $8 million and was satisfied with the result. I felt we had provided minimal value.

(2) We worked for a seller who would only sell to a buyer who would hire all of the employees and maintain the seller's obsolete facility. This not only reduced the number of potential buyers but also eliminated virtually all of the synergies which exist in a consolidation. The sale price was rather low, but our client, the seller, was very satisfied. Once again I felt we had provided minimal value.

(3) We worked with a company that wanted to sell for a very high value. We completed an appraisal and market valuation and told them that they should go back to work for a couple of years, improve their business and then market it. This they did. We marketed the business, received exceptional competition from several major buyers, and sold at a top price. This time both our firm and our client believed we provided substantial value.

Qualitatively, it is relatively easy for us to measure our value. When we complete a project and a client believes we did a fine job, would want to work with us in the future, and would welcome the chance to give us a good reference, then we have provided value.

A few generalities about successful companies: All companies make many mistakes. But a company will likely be profitable and provide real value if it does the most important things right. Really successful companies do the few most important things right again and again.

A couple was checking out of a resort, and the husband noticed that the bill was twice the $200 per night that he had expected. He confronted the hotel clerk who explained the room indeed was only $200 per night - but the golf course and the exercise room cost extra.

The husband asked, "Did I use the golf course?"
The clerk answered, "No, but it was available."
The husband continued, "Did I use the exercise room?" and the clerk once again answered, "No, but it was available."

The husband thought for a moment and then said, "Well, I think you owe me $200."
The clerk asked, "Why?"

The husband asked, "Did you have sex with my wife?"
The clerk said, "No!"
The husband replied, "Well, she was available!"

To Satisfy Your Customers --- Your Bill Should Match Their Expectations

Your customers want value! They want to know what they are getting for their money. Be careful to clarify what they can expect to receive from you and be sure they understand. Otherwise they can become dissatisfied and discouraged while working with you. Don't present them with a hotel bill with additional features that are expensive and unidentified unless you know that they actually received what they requested; and, if you want to collect all of the monies due you, advise your customers in advance and put it in writing.

A man went to a consultant about a debt that he owed but didn't want to pay.

The consultant suggested that the man pay, and told the man that it will cost $50 for his advice.

The man said, "I'm not taking your advice."

If You Provide A Service --- Be Sure They Pay Whether Or Not They Heed Your Advice

If you are a consultant giving advice, you should recognize that many people will only accept what they want to hear and will give no serious consideration to your expertise. So, be sure to get paid something in advance to protect yourself from those who might not be interested in taking your advice.

Illustration by Jared Martin

I'm not taking your advice.

A violin player from the city orchestra came home late at night to find a squadron of police cars outside his house. The Chief of Police met him at the driveway.

"I am afraid I have some terrible news for you," said the Chief. "While you were out, the orchestra conductor came to your house, stole all the contents, and burned it down."

The violin player said. "You must be kidding. The conductor came to my house!"

If You Contribute Effectively --- The Conductor Will Invite You To His House

When you work hard, you rightfully expect to be recognized. Life rarely works out that way, and more commonly even your best efforts are ignored. This is just how things work in business and life. But, if you keep at it, and improve your ability to communicate your efforts and successes properly, you increase your chances of proper recognition, and the odds improve that the conductor will invite you to dinner at his house and not burn yours.

A man was traveling with his girlfriend in New York. They came upon a store which had a beautiful dress in the window, and the man took a brick and threw it at the window. He reached through the broken window and stole the dress for his girlfriend.

They continued walking, and the girlfriend saw a gorgeous mink coat in another store window. The man picked up another brick, broke the window, and handed the mink coat to his girlfriend.

They walked on, and the girlfriend eyed a diamond ring in the window. She admired the ring, and asked the man if he could get that for her.

The man looked at her, and said, "Honey, what do you think I am, made of bricks?"

A Customer Can Always Surprise You --- Because You Never Know When They Will Run Out Of Bricks

Most customers repeat behaviors. Their past actions become the best clues to their future actions. But clues don't eliminate surprises, and your customer will stop buying when he runs out of bricks.

A doctor woke up in the middle of the night and discovered that a pipe in his basement had burst and there was water all over the floor. He called his plumber and described his problem. The plumber said to him, "Doc, it is 3:00 in the morning. Here's what you should do now: Put two aspirin in the water pipe, and call me in the morning."*

Make House Calls --- Or You'll Find Yourself With Aspirin In Your Water Pipes

As a salesman, it is virtually impossible to contribute too much. Providing extra service is the basis of your job. Make house calls! Your customers don't want aspirin in their water pipes.

---

* An alternative to this joke is the following story:

A man called his doctor's office for an appointment. "I'm sorry," said the receptionist, "We can't fit you in for at least two weeks."

"But I could be dead by then."

"No problem. If your wife lets us know, we'll cancel the appointment."

A teacher wanted her students to learn how to spell and how to use words as a practical part of life. So she asked her students if each would write down what his father did, spell his occupation and give an example.

The first student said that her father was a baker, spelled b-a-k-e-r, and that her father could bring cookies to the class and give one to each student.

The second said her father was a banker, spelled b-a-n-k-e-r, and that her father could come to school and give each of her friends $1.

Next, the teacher pointed to Joey who said that his father was an electrician, spelled, e-l-e-k... and then Joey continued trying to spell electrician, but each time he was unsuccessful. The teacher told Joey to sit down and think about it, and said she was sure he could come up with the correct spelling of electrician.

The next student said, "My father is a bookie, spelled, b-o-o-k-i-e, and, he will give you 8 to 5 odds that Joey will never be able to spell electrician."

Be Careful With Whom You Bet --- Some Day Joey Will Be Able To Spell Electrician

Take the bet: The odds are very high that, with time, Joey will be able to spell "electrician." This is especially true if you share the potential benefits with Joey to encourage his efforts. *

---

* Suggested by my son, David.

Once again Harry's wife told about her dream: "Harry, last night I dreamed that you bought me a mink coat and you know how happy that made me."

This was a recurrent dream, and since Harry knew that his chances of affording a mink coat were slim, he usually said nothing when his wife described her mink coat dream. This time, he thought a moment, and said, "Dear, tonight when you are dreaming, dream that you are wearing it in good health!"

All Customers Dream Of Mink Coats --- And Good Health

Your dreams will come true when you are able to help others realize their dreams. You must convince your clients that they will get two mink coats if you expect your wife to receive one.

Illustration by Carole Pollack

...dream that you are wearing it in good health.

For a long time, a psychiatrist provided therapy for a patient who believed that he was Romeo. One day the man came to the psychiatrist with a surprise. "Doctor," he announced, "I no longer believe that I am Romeo!"

"That is wonderful," said the doctor, "And what is the first thing you did after you discovered that you were not Romeo?"

"Well," said the patient, "I called Juliet and told her!"

Work With Your Crazy Customers --- And Help Them Find Their Juliets

Most people don't change at all; some people change slowly; all good salesmen learn to adapt rapidly. Therefore, don't expect great changes in others. Your goals are to change their thoughts, which can only be accomplished by altering their emotional environment. To help a customer you must help him find his Juliet.

George and Mary celebrated their 15th anniversary by going to the French Riviera for a 2-week vacation. While they were there, they rented a cottage, complete with butler and maid. After a wonderful trip, they returned home.

Several months later George received a letter, and became upset. Mary asked, "George, what is the problem? We've been married for 15 years. Your problems are my problems. My troubles are your troubles."

George looked at her and said, "Mary, you are right! Let me tell you what has happened. Remember the trip on the Riviera? Well, the maid is pregnant, and Mary, you are right, we are to blame!"

If You Can't Convince The Buyer --- You Are Both To Blame

A truly outstanding salesman continually strives to understand his customer's problems. His problems are your problems. You will be successful if you treat every situation as if you are both pregnant.

In Serbia, the Montenegrins are reputed to be less than hard workers and the following is typical of a Montenegrin joke. *

A young man was applying for a job in Montenegro and asked about the hours for work.

The owner told him, "On the weekends there is no work. On Monday, there is no work because we are resting from the weekend. On Tuesday there is no work because we are preparing for Wednesday. On Wednesday we work. On Thursday we rest from the work on Wednesday and there is no work. On Friday we prepare for the weekend and there is no work."

The young man looked at the owner and asked, "Do we have to work every Wednesday?"

You Will Never Be Successful --- If You Don't Work Every Wednesday

The most successful people I know don't believe they are entitled to anything, don't complain or blame others and just go about life figuring out what is important to them and doing it. Instead of asking for help, they figure out what is necessary to succeed and make do with the resources they have. They also work every Wednesday.

* Told to me by Desko Mikitovic, Consul General, Republic of Serbia, Chicago.

"When I was young," said Don, "my first job was selling life insurance. My prospects sometimes accused me of not being interested in their needs and only wanting to help myself. I told them that they were wrong; and, in fact, 'I don't want to sell life insurance to everyone. I only want to sell to those who love their families and want to prepare for their future.'"*

To Want Success Is Not To Be Greedy ---After All You Are Only Helping Those Who Love Their Families

As Jerome Kern said about his music, "Stay uncommercial. There is a lot of money in it."

Don't let your prospects allow you to think that you are too greedy. You are just like everyone else, and you are doing what is good for your family. Your family must buy groceries too.

---

* Told to me by Don Allen, my college friend.

Years ago telephone calls were handled by live operators who connected all phone calls. Early in 1946, Hans called his dad from college and asked for $500.

Dad said, "The telephone line is bad and I can't hear you."

At this point the operator joined the conversation and commented, "There is nothing wrong with the line. I can hear you both perfectly clear."

Dad said, "Well, if you can hear him so well, why don't you give him the $500?" *

Time Your Comments Carefully --- Or It May Cost You $500

You will find in business that there are many folks who want to take your ideas and not pay for them. They will have you spend your money, your time, your ideas, tell you "thank you very much;" and then they will use your ideas and not pay.   If this happens to you once, then the next time you deal with them, remind them that you don't have to share your ideas and spend your money, energy and time to make them a profit unless they pay your fee.

So, even though you believe the telephone line is perfectly clear, you may want to learn a bit more before you contribute your thought --- or, it could cost you $500.

---

* Red Strangland, *Norwegian Home Companion*, Barnes and Noble Books, NY 1987, pg. 114

When a young girl asked her mother how old she was, the mother wouldn't say. The daughter then asked how much her mother weighed and the mother wouldn't say. Finally she asked her mother why she got a divorce, and, once again, the mother wouldn't say.

At school the next day, the young girl asked a friend what to do. The friend said that she should go into her mother's wallet and find the driver's license.

The girl found the wallet and read the driver's license. Then she told her mom that she knew her mom was 34 years old, and weighed 144 pounds. Mom was surprised. Finally, the daughter said she knew why Mom got divorced. This time, Mom asked, "Why?"

"Because you got an 'F' in sex."

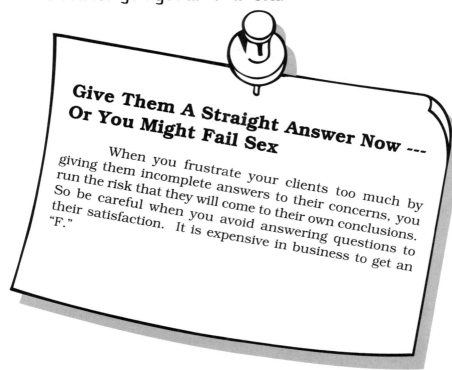

Give Them A Straight Answer Now --- Or You Might Fail Sex

When you frustrate your clients too much by giving them incomplete answers to their concerns, you run the risk that they will come to their own conclusions. So be careful when you avoid answering questions to their satisfaction. It is expensive in business to get an "F."

A woman saw two black hearses followed by an extremely large dog next to a woman. Behind them were several hundred women walking in line.

She walked up to the woman and said, "What is going on here?"

The woman replied, "In the first hearse is my husband. In the second hearse is my mother-in-law."

"Why," asked the inquirer, "is the large dog here?"

"Oh," said the woman, "he killed them both!"

"Where can I get a dog like that?"

"Get in line!"

Some Relationships Are Best To Avoid --- Although You Might Prefer To Use A Killer Dog

Admittedly, the joke goes to the extreme of what to do if your spouse and in-laws are irritating you. When the relationship is very bad, it will require great effort, time and expense to figure out how to improve it (or whether it can be improved). Your responsibility is to make a great effort to think about and understand the situation and possibly to seek advice as to how to improve the relationship. If you have children, it is worth more effort, time and expense; otherwise every one of your future holidays can be a trying experience.

In business, there will be some people you will not care about, and you might even wish them destroyed by a large dog. All you can do is try to understand them and try to work with them --- and if that doesn't work, then get in line with those who avoid them.

Illustration by Alex Wohlrab

Get in line!

A man loved his dog. When the dog died, the man decided to give the dog a traditional religious funeral. When he went to a rabbi and asked the rabbi to perform the burial service, the rabbi said, "He is a dog. We only allow burial services for **people** who have died."

The man then went to a priest and asked the priest to perform the burial service. The priest also said, "He is a dog. We only allow burial services for **people** who have died."

In desperation, he went to an Episcopal minister and asked the minister to perform the burial service. But, once again, the minister said, "He is a dog. We only perform burial services for **people** who have died."

Then the dog owner said, "But I was going to donate $10,000 to your Church for the service."

The minister replied, "Why didn't you tell me your dog was an **Episcopalian** dog?"

To Obtain The Services You Seek --- Clearly Explain What Type Of Dog You Have

There are many reasons why customers don't act but should act as you would like them to. Your challenge is to clarify for them why it is in their best interest to agree with you. So, if you are selling, be sure to clarify what type of dog you are selling.

A little girl moved into town, and for the first time she visited her neighbor. When she was about to leave for home, the neighbor said, "You must come again soon. We would like to see more of you."

The little girl replied, "But there isn't any more of me."

Customers Want More From You — They Don't Want To See More Of You

Genuine business success generally depends more on substance than frequency. Most executives are genuinely busy: they don't want to see more of you; they want more from you.

A fellow went to a bookstore and asked for a book on speed-reading. The clerk found one and said, "This will cut your reading time in half."

"Fine," said the customer, "I'll take two!"

Customers Play The Angles --- They Always Want Double

People don't appreciate your speed-reading, your knowledge, your wisdom. Therefore, don't teach them speed-reading. Find out what they read, and read that book.

At Christmas time a woman invited the mailman into her home. She said, "Please come in and have breakfast." They had a wonderful breakfast together, and afterward, as the mailman was about to leave, she invited him to come up to her bedroom. They undressed and had wonderful sex together. Just before he left, she handed him $2.

He couldn't believe his good fortune and asked her to explain what was happening. She said, "I spoke to my husband and asked him what I should give you for Christmas. My husband said, 'Screw the mailman and give him 2 bucks!'"

"But," she added, "Breakfast was my idea."

Customers Need Room For Their Thoughts --- Let Breakfast Be Their Idea

Customers often have the ability to solve their problems without your help. To be successful, it is usually best to guide your customers passively so that both the ideas and the conclusions are theirs. Your major concern is that their conclusions are consistent with your goals. Leave room for their thoughts — let breakfast be their idea.

One Autumn, an Italian, a Frenchman and a Slovak were about to be executed by a firing squad and they were told they had one wish.

The Italian asked for pizza, got his pizza and was executed.

The Frenchmen asked for filet mignon, got his filet mignon and was executed.

The Slovak asked for Strawberries.

"Strawberries???"

"Strawberries are out of season."

"So, I'll wait."

Timing Is Important --- If There Are No Strawberries, Be Prepared To Wait

There are no permanent good customers or bad customers. There is only timing when your product or service is needed or not needed. Your goal is to sell your product or service during your strawberry season or to convince them to wait until the strawberry season arrives.

So, I'll wait!

Three elderly men were talking.

"When I was young, I would wake up at 7 o'clock, urinate fully in 30 seconds; and now I work for an hour and can barely get a trickle," said the first.

The second complained, "When I was a young man, I would wake up at 7 o'clock, complete a full bowel movement within 5 minutes; and now, if I have a small bowel movement once a week, I am happy!"

The third elderly man entered the conversation, and said, "At 7 o'clock in the morning I have no problem. I urinate like Niagara Falls, and I have a regular bowel movement immediately. My problem is that I don't wake up until 9 o'clock."

All Customers Have Problems --- Even If They Sleep Until 9 o'clock

For all important business activities three steps are identified by these questions:

(1) What is our Goal?
(2) What Performance is necessary to achieve the goal?
(3) What is the Timing?

Of the three, Timing is the one that gets the least attention and therefore often represents the reason why we fail. When to talk to those who have a need to know, and when to present information is significant. When to ask for money and when to give up on an account are also questions of timing that too frequently are not addressed. So, if you really want to be successful, hold off your implementation until you have verified that the timing is right for your customer.

Sam and Joe were talking because Sam had a very serious drinking problem. Joe said, "Everything is completely the fault of the alcohol."

Sam replied, "I am so glad you said that, Joe. You are the only one who puts the fault where it truly lies. Everyone else tells me it's my problem."

Your Goal Is To Help Your Customers With Their Business Problems --- and To Help Them Feel Good About Themselves

Remember that in your business dealings, your problems don't count. Your customers' non-business problems don't count. Only your customers' business problems count.

If a personal matter appears, it almost always helps to show your customers kindness and sympathy toward their personal issues, but your efforts should be directed toward their business actions so that they are consistent with your goals. No reason to correct their personal actions: if they think the fault is completely the alcohol, let the issue rest and let it be the fault of the alcohol.

A man was sentenced to 15 years in prison for armed robbery, and during his first day he noticed a small fly in his prison cell. He decided that for his long-term project he would make this fly into an exceptional fly. For the first 5 years he worked with the fly but was unable to train it even to turn on its back.

During the next 5 years, he made a bit of progress and in 10 years the fly learned how to respond to virtually any verbal direction. On command, it could fly in patterns, including zigging and zagging and figure 8's.

On the day of his release from prison, the man went to a bar to celebrate. He brought his fly with him so he could impress the bar tender, and he said, "Bartender, do you see this fly?"

The bartender looked over and squashed the fly with a powerful right hand, saying, "We get too many flies like this in here!"

Your Idea Won't Fly --- Until You Clarify Its Value

In business negotiations one can learn a great deal from the questions both sides ask. Try to think about the reasons for each question. Is it strictly for information, or rhetorical? Is the questioner trying to make a point by asking the question? Does the question support doing the deal or is it posed to quash it?

Also, it is important that you be careful with the questions you raise. If you are just out of prison and have trained your fly for 15 years, instead of asking, "Do you see this fly?" you might want to ask, "Isn't this a miraculous fly that I trained for 15 years?"

A song writer's son, a writer's son, and a preacher's son were talking about their fathers. The songwriter's son said, "My father can write a tune in an hour and sell it the next day for $500."

The writer's son said, "My father can write a story in an hour and sell it to the Reader's Digest for $2,000."

The preacher's son looked up and said, "You know, when my father gives a sermon, it takes half an hour, and then ten men carry the money up to him."

You have Not Reached Your Potential Until Ten Men Are Required To Carry The Money Up To You

A fascinating aspect of life is our inability to maximize our skills. Don't think you have achieved your potential until it requires ten men to carry the money you earn for a half-hour speech.

Bob, Joe and Bert were discussing the greatest inventions of all time.

Bob said that the computer was the greatest: it promoted the development of communications, transfer of information and led toward modern society.

Joe suggested the wheel. Even though it was thousands of years old, it led to virtually every major mechanical invention, including the automobile.

"No, no!" said Bert. "The greatest invention of all time is the thermos bottle!"

The others looked at him in disbelief and Bob asked, "What is so remarkable about a thermos bottle? All it does is keep hot things hot and cold things cold."

"Yes," said Bert, "but how does it know?"

Accept The Fact That Your Customers Will Run Hot And Cold --- Like The Amazing Thermos

Is our customer hot or cold? Can we match our mood and behavior to his internal temperatures? Can we pitch our own excitement to match his outlook, thus equating the intensity of our pitch to the intensity of his interest? If we accomplish these things we will have a full thermos.

Janet entered a butcher shop and was told that the cost of roast beef was $15 a pound. She looked at the butcher, outraged, and told him that usually she bought roast beef down the block from Sam who charged only $10 a pound.

"The reason I am in this store is that today Sam is out of roast beef," Janet said. "So why should I pay you $15?"

The butcher looked at her and said, "Ma'am, when we are out of roast beef, it's only $2 a pound!"

Always Seek Alternatives --- But Accept The Fact That Sometimes The Best Alternative Is To Buy Roast Beef For $15 A Pound

One of the challenges of life is to decide what to do when you can't get what you want. When Sam is out of roast beef, there is no way you can buy roast beef from Sam. In business dealings, you often must find an alternative to your first choice. In negotiations, this is referred to as BATNA (the Best Alternative To a Negotiated Agreement). In the case above, the customer needs an alternative to her first choice (roast beef at $10 a pound) and thus needs a BATNA. If she doesn't want to pay $15 per pound for roast beef, she should consider getting an alternative like perhaps pastrami. Besides, a good pastrami is better than roast beef!

This page is intentionally left blank
So please don't read this page.

A mother and her son were looking for a missing contact lens. The son gave up. The mother kept looking until she found it.

"I really looked hard for that, Mom," said the boy. "How did you manage to find it?"

Mom replied, "We weren't looking for the same thing. You were looking for a small piece of plastic. I was looking for $150."

Value Is In The Eye Of The Beholder --- Your Customer May Not Value Your Piece Of Plastic At $150

In dealing with customers, learn their priorities. Otherwise you will be looking for a piece of plastic when they are looking for $150.

Groucho Marx once visited a man who owned a house with a magnificent view of the Pacific Ocean and who bragged about the beauty. When he asked Groucho what he thought of the view, Groucho commented, "Don't think much of it. Take away the ocean and what do you have?"

Concentrate On What You Do Best --- Find Your Ocean View

For every business there is usually one thing that it does exceptionally well; something that it does best. For example, at our firm, we believe we do a good job evaluating businesses in our field so that our client will have a realistic view of his business and provide a buyer with an objective view of its attributes and value.

My suggestion is to identify your business's major strength, whether it is a skill, a location, or an experience. Identify and define your special excellence and build upon it. Your special ability can't be taken from you, just as the ocean view cannot be removed from a beautiful house.

Illustration by Alex Wohlrab

Take away the ocean, and what do you have?

Chapter 4
ASSUMPTIONS

Scientific principles may be absolute, but most business truths are relative because they are almost always based on incomplete information. All business decisions require assumptions. In general, the more difficult the decision, the more uncertainty and the greater the assumption(s). Our prejudices compound the risks while blinding us to objective evaluation of the decision. We can reduce the uncertainly related to our assumptions by asking questions, getting other opinions, and matching how our assumptions meet our basic values.

For example, at our firm we recently considered a new account that appeared to have excellent technology for treating prostate problems, and several investors had expressed an initial interest in supporting the company. However, it became clear that the CEO held strong convictions about how we should do our job and was not a good listener.

Let's look at the assumptions that we made in deciding whether to take the account:

(1) The technology is strong and likely to be effective;

(2) The market is large and significant;

(3) The company needs a lot of investment money and it would be a large deal for us; and

(4) The manager would likely be difficult to work with.

So, we had to make a determination: If we work for this company, will the CEO listen to us and work with us? Can we adapt to work effectively together? Might he modify his behavior?

Our decision went back to our values, and working for people who respect our expertise and allow us to do our job is a critical value to us. So, we decided not to take on the project. We concluded that the leader probably would be too difficult and that we should look elsewhere for business.

103

Sam and Sadie had been married for many years. One day Sam went shopping by himself to buy some clothing, but could find nothing he wanted until he came upon a shoe store and purchased a fabulous pair of alligator shoes.

He wore the new shoes home and asked Sadie to look at him and see if she noticed what was different. She said, "I don't notice anything different about your appearance. You are wearing the same weary, old pants and shirt."

He took off his pants and shirt and, to make it easy for Sadie to notice, he removed all of his clothing except his new alligator shoes.

When he asked her again if she saw anything different, she replied, (looking at his private parts) "I don't notice anything different about your appearance. It is hanging down, as usual."

"Take another look," he requested, and once again she replied, "No. It still hangs down."

Disappointed, he said, "Look at my shoes. What do you think of my new alligator shoes?"

She responded, "You should have bought a hat."

It May Be Obvious To You --- But You Still Should Consider Buying A Hat

The obvious is not always the obvious.* Whenever we are highly focused on anything, we increase the possibility of overlooking the obvious. At the first sign that someone else sees things differently, seek to find what is important to them; after all, when another's mind is focused elsewhere, the most effective way to get serious attention to your problem is usually to address theirs first. Sam and Sadie can both look at the same information, come to different conclusions and both be right. However, I believe that most men, if they thought it over, would have been better off buying a hat!

* Thanks to Steve Weinstein for this obvious comment.

When Muhammad Ali was a kid in Louisville, KY, someone stole his brand-new bicycle. He reported it to the police and told the policeman who wrote up the report that if he found the guy who stole the bike he would beat him up. Muhammad never found the thief but every time he got into the ring, he looked across at the other fighter and told himself, "Hey, that's the guy who stole my bicycle."

Customers May Overreact If They Think You Stole Their Bike

When a client or customer becomes annoyed and attacks you angrily, it is natural to assume that you are somewhat responsible. However, many times his anger has little to do with you. It is often best, when a customer is angry, to let him talk it out. Ask questions to clarify his concern, and determine what, if any, relationship you have to his problem. After all, he must first determine whether you stole his bike or whether he just **thinks** you stole his bike.

In 1960, for the first time in three decades, a rural farmer went to the city and decided to see a movie. The movie cost $2 and the popcorn $1.50. The farmer commented to the popcorn vendor, "The last time I came to a movie, the movie cost 25 cents and the popcorn was only 10 cents."

The vendor replied, "You're really going to enjoy the movie. We have sound and color now."

Be Kind --- Accept The Fact That Old Folks Don't Know New Stuff

When I was 35 and my folks were 60, I thought this was a particularly funny joke. I viewed the challenges for the elderly to adjust to change as humorous and underestimated the respect, kindness and sympathy they deserved. Now that I am older, when I see rapid technological change, I better appreciate how comforting it must have been to go to a movie for a quarter, buy popcorn for a dime and not be concerned that the movies were in black and white and didn't have sound.

We have sound and color now.

A man was told that everyone in town was having sex with his wife. Men would call his wife, make a date, pay $5, and have some fun.

The husband started laughing when he heard this. He explained, "All of these guys are paying $5? I get it for free!"

If You Make A Great Deal, Don't Feel Bad For The Other Guy --- The Other Guy May Get It For Free

If you believe that you have gotten the best of a business deal, don't feel bad if it appears to be too one-sided. If you have gotten each point of the negotiation to proceed your way, enjoy it. The other guy may get it for free.

A man and a nun were riding on a camel, about two days' ride from Cairo, Egypt, when the camel died.

The nun looked at the man and asked, "Since we're in the desert with no water and sure to die, I would like to ask you to take off your clothes because I have never seen a man naked and I would like to see that before I die."

The man took off his clothes and when the nun asked what his private part was for, he responded, "If I take that and stick it into you, I can create life."

The nun looked at him and said, "Well, why don't you stick it in the camel, and let's get going?"

Explain Things Carefully --- Or You May Be Asked To Stick It In The Camel

One of the most difficult parts of communication is to discover the knowledge level of your customer and to reconcile your customer's knowledge with your own. Invariably, you and your customer come from different knowledge bases in more respects than either of you acknowledge.

Your primary goal is to make your customers feel comfortable so that they will discuss more readily their thoughts and ideas. This will help clarify their knowledge level.

Many times this is difficult to achieve because it requires much skill, experience and often more time than either of you are willing to spend. Sometimes, their lack of knowledge is very easy to discover, like when they suggest you stick it in the camel.

Recently, I read about a mother who reported the following incident:

"I was driving with my three young children one warm summer evening when a woman in the convertible ahead of us stood up and waved. She was stark naked! As I was reeling from the shock, I heard my 5-year-old shout from the back seat, 'Mom! That lady isn't wearing a seat belt!'"

Accept Diversity Of Thought --- Some Folks Would Rather Drive Naked Than Wear Seat Belts

Different people make different assumptions about the same event because they have different backgrounds, different genes and different priorities. People will tend to focus on their knowledge and prejudices. One of your highest goals should be to find out what they assume. You can usually accomplish this by encouraging them to speak. Remember that many young folks have been taught that wearing a seat belt is more significant than being dressed while driving.

Illustration by Abby Marten

Mom! That lady isn't wearing a seat belt!

A young boy saw a Harley Davidson* motorcycle, became excited and told his dad, "Look at that beautiful bike. I'm going to get one of those someday."

"That will happen over my dead body," said the father.

The boy went to his mother and said, "Great news! I'm going to get a Harley as soon as Dad dies."

If You Don't Want Your Kid To Get A Bike --- Just Say "Never"

Each of us has a unique perspective. One man's poison is another man's opportunity. There are so many ways to fail and so many ways to succeed. So, be careful when you explain to your kid the circumstances under which he might get a bike!

---

* When a person lives in Milwaukee, Harley Davidson is the only choice for a motorcycle.

A husband fed the birds all day. He did this every day. One day his wife asked him why he fed the birds all the time.

He said, "Who knows? In my next life I may come back as a bird."

She asked, "What? Again?" *

Make Room For Nonsense --- You May Come Back As A Bird.**

Everything doesn't have to make sense nor does it have to have a reason. As Khalil Gibran wrote in *The Prophet*, "For reason, ruling alone, is a force confining; and passion, unattended, is a flame that burns to its own destruction."

There is room in life for nonsense. Much great humor borders on nonsense and yet provides real insight into humanity. So, the next time a guy feeds you nonsense, just treat it as a piece of life and don't be too critical. Perhaps he will come back as a bird. Again.

---

* Another nonsensical joke I like but could not think of what to say about it is this: I called my psychic friend who asked why I was calling. I said, "You tell me."

** A final nonsensical joke: A friend asked the mullah how old are you? "Forty," replied the mullah. The friend said, "But you said the same thing two years ago."
"Yes," replied the mullah, "I always stand by what I have said."

Probably you have not called the Psychiatric Hotline, but if you do, this is the greeting you will receive:

I am the operator from the Psychiatric Hotline:

If you are obsessive-compulsive, please press 1 repeatedly.
If you are co-dependent, ask someone to press 2.
If you have multiple personalities, please press 3, 4, 5 and 6.
If you are paranoid-delusional, we know who you are and what you want. Just stay on the line until we can trace the call.
If you are schizophrenic, listen carefully and a little voice will tell you which number to press.
If you are manic-depressive, it doesn't matter which number you press. No one will answer.

Be Realistic --- Recognize That You Are Probably Just As Crazy As Your Customers

Most customers believe they are normal and that, should a dispute arise, it is you that has the mental problem of not being able to see it their way. You believe, of course, that it is they who have the problem because of their inability to see things your way, which of course is rational thinking.

Experience teaches that there is no universal normal behavior and that what is appropriate in one circumstance generates problems in another. To be a successful sales person you want to adjust your behavior to best suit the situation.

All successful sales people are crazy in one way or another --- and your goal is to be crazy in the most effective way.

James was walking with Martin past a ferocious dog. James was afraid of the dog, but Martin cautioned him not to worry because the dog was barking.

Martin said, "You know the old proverb, 'Barking dogs never bite.'"

"Yes," said James. "You know that barking dogs never bite. I know that barking dogs never bite. The important question is whether the dog knows."

Remember That Your Best Customer, Like A Dog --- Can Bite

For every business matter there is a decision process and a decision maker. If you work hard to understand the process and find out who the decision maker is, you have multiplied your chances for success. A decision in your favor by someone without decision making authority is almost meaningless. So, to be successful, find out who is the barking dog and find out under what circumstances he bites.

While excavating an ancient tomb in Egypt, two archeologists found an urn containing food to nourish the dead upon their reawakening. Curious about certain engravings on the urn, they called a professor of hieroglyphics, who gave this translation: "Best if used before 2000 B.C."

Rules Are Man-Made, Often Unnecessary --- And Many Should Have Expired Before 2000 B.C.

Rules are man-made and many make very little sense. To be successful you must distinguish between them. Many should be eliminated: For example, it is 2 a.m. and you are driving. You get to a red light and there is no one around for as far as you can see. The law requires you to stop. But why should you? You are wasting gas and time and no one is benefiting from your stopping. My Uncle Jess used to say that illegal U-turns were only illegal if someone was looking. He may or may not have been right – but it is certainly true that many rules should have expired before 2000 B.C.

Illustration by Ryan Carter

Best if used before 2000 B.C.

Golfer Lee Trevino was questioned, "Do you feel pressure when you're on the last hole of a tournament and you're putting for $1 million?"

"That's not pressure," Trevino answered. "Real pressure is when you're playing somebody for $10 and you only have $5 in your pocket."

A Person's Financial Resources Determines His Definition Of What Is Expensive

As F. Scott Fitzgerald said, "The rich are different from you and me," and the fact is that, in many ways, rich people behave differently from poor people. Although this comment may be politically incorrect, I have found that the rich and the very rich tend to make more decisions themselves and want your ideas primarily for support or background. For these folks, asking questions and guiding the process with questions can be very effective.

On the other hand, those who have not made their financial mark yet tend to be more receptive to financial and business suggestions. For these folks, it is usually more effective to offer solutions to their problems. This comment should surprise no one, because it is natural for people with $1 million cash in the bank to act differently than those with $5 in their pocket.

Illustration by Abby Marten

I wish I had $10.

A fellow was trying to impress a new acquaintance with the contributions his family made. "My great-great-grandfather fought with George Washington. My great-grandfather fought with Jackson at the battle of New Orleans. My grandfather fought in the Civil War under Grant. My father fought in the First World War with Pershing, and I fought with Eisenhower in the Second World War," he said.

Said the acquaintance, "Apparently your family can't get along with anybody."

No Matter How Loveable You Are ---Some will Claim That You Can't Get Along With Anybody

Good salesmen learn early that the meanings of words often don't match their intentions. Look at your client while you are talking and sense what he is feeling. What he is feeling will guide you to what he is thinking — and what he is thinking is more important than what he is saying.

A very attractive woman checked into a most expensive and deluxe New York City hotel. As she started to get undressed, she noticed that there was a window washer outside, and she decided that she would have some fun. While he was washing her window, she started to undo her blouse.

The window washer nonchalantly continued washing the window. At this point, she continued disrobing until her top half was naked. He continued washing.

Because her charms were being ignored, she continued until completely naked. Once again there was no response. Finally, she walked directly to the window and glared at him.

He looked at her and said, "What's wrong, Lady? Haven't you ever seen a window washer before?"

Don't Assume That They Have Never Seen A Window Washer

There is always a balance to be struck between treating others as if they are stupid and giving them credit for knowledge they don't possess. Your understanding of their understanding should be constantly fine-tuned and balanced. Some people have never seen a window washer. Some people have never seen a naked lady. Most have never seen a naked lady window washer.

Scott walked into church in a small parish. The preacher's sermon to the congregation concerned fire, brimstone and death. "All of you who live in this parish have sinned. All of you who live in this parish will die," he declared.

Scott started to laugh, and the preacher angrily asked why he was laughing.

Scott replied, "I am laughing because I don't live in this parish."

If You Threaten People --- Be Sure They Live In Your Parish

When you are negotiating from a position of strength, there is a tendency to overreach. Overreaching only works when the other side acknowledges your power and behaves accordingly. The results will be very bad if the other side does not accept your aggressiveness. So, before you present your doomsday picture of fire and brimstone, find out first if the other person lives in your parish.

Illustration by Janelle Crawford

I don't live in this parish.

A Chinaman and a Jew were arguing. "You Chinese cannot be trusted. Ever since Pearl Harbor I have not trusted the Chinese people," said the Jew.

The Chinaman replied, "What do you mean, Chinese? Those were the Japanese who attacked at Pearl Harbor. The Chinese had nothing to do with it."

The Jew replied, "Chinese! Japanese! Same thing!"

Now, the Chinaman started to complain and said, "I haven't trusted the Jewish people since the Titanic was sunk!"

The Jew didn't believe his ears and exclaimed, "The Jews had nothing to do with the sinking of the Titanic. Don't you remember? That was an iceberg!"

The Chinaman looked at him and said, "Iceberg, Goldberg, Greenberg. Same thing!"

Small Differences Create Important Distinctions --- Chinese And Japanese Are Not The Same Thing

It has been said that a person often thinks he is thinking, but he is really rearranging his prejudices. We are all prejudiced in some ways and prejudiced against in some ways. The trick is not to deny it – but not to be defined by it. Many Americans are prejudiced against both Japanese and Chinese and sometimes against Goldbergs and Greenbergs. Few are prejudiced against icebergs.

Andrew was walking down the street in New York and he noticed a panhandler shaking his cup. Andrew put a quarter into the cup, walked down the street, looked back and saw that the panhandler had taken off his dark eyeshades and had removed the quarter from the cup. So he walked back to the beggar and said, "I thought you were blind."

The beggar looked at him and said, "I am just a substitute for the regular beggar on this corner who is off today. I am the deaf mute."

Deal With The Decision-maker --- Or You Will Be Less Effective Than A Deaf Mute

There is usually one key decision maker. Find him. Only by getting his attention can you be effective. Trying to sell a non-key decision-maker may succeed, but it is as difficult as trying to spot a deaf mute.

Diane went to a psychiatrist and complained, "Doctor, I am crazy!"

The psychiatrist replied, "I have listened to you very carefully for several sessions now, and I'm convinced that there is absolutely nothing wrong with you and that you are mentally sound. Why do you think you're crazy?"

Diane replied, "Because I like pancakes."

The psychiatrist looked at her and said, "So what. I like them too. In fact, I love pancakes."

Diane arose and said, "That's wonderful. Would you like some? I have a truckload of pancakes just outside."

Before You Agree --- Make Sure You Know How Much They Like Pancakes

Listen! Question! Learn! Don't make any important decision until you learn how much they like pancakes.

Illustration by Dana Borremans

I have a truckload of pancakes just outside.

A supermarket manager noticed that one of his customers purchased only dog food.

One day he stopped the man and said, "Listen, I am not going to allow you to purchase any more dog food unless you prove to me that you have a dog. I am worried that you are purchasing this dog food to eat yourself because it is so cheap." A week later the man returned with a large poodle, and when the manager saw the dog, he decided that the man could rightfully purchase dog food.

A few weeks later the customer returned and started to purchase cat food. Once again, the manager was suspicious and advised the customer that unless he could prove that he owned a cat, he could not purchase more cat food. Sure enough, the next week when the customer returned, he brought a small Siamese, thus verifying he was entitled to cat food.

Some time elapsed, and the customer returned carrying a brown bag. The manager ran over and stuck his hand in the bag and discovered that it contained nothing but shit. The store manager removed his hand in disgust and asked, "What did you do that for?"

The customer answered, "I wanted to purchase five rolls of toilet paper." *

Don't Hassle Them --- If They Want To Buy Toilet Paper

In business, truth and proof are not fixed points. The best business leaders often say to themselves, "I know there are many good reasons for not doing this; however, on balance it is our best option, and so we are going to go ahead." Once a leader makes a decision, his full energies are devoted toward implementation. No second guessing is allowed. He goes on to the next decision. He does not recheck his decision by sticking his hands into brown bags filled with uncertainty.

* From my late uncle, Jess Marks.

Mark picked up his shirt from the commercial laundry and discovered that it was spotted and could no longer be used. He returned it and complained.

The owner of the laundry said, "It was not my fault. Your shirt was no good. What do you expect me to do?"

Mark said, "I want my money back." And then he pointed to the sign which read, "MONEY CHEERFULLY REFUNDED IF NOT SATISFIED."

The owner looked at the customer and said, "But there was nothing wrong with your money, AND I AM VERY SATISFIED."

Remember That Your Company's Money Is Always Easy To Spend --- And Difficult To Get Back

Before you purchase anything significant, learn about the obstacles to reversing the transaction and getting your money back. Just because you didn't like your shirt does not mean that he didn't like your money.

Robert purchased a new Rolls Royce and decided that he would impress his friend, Larry. He drove up to Larry's house, invited him for a ride, and off they went.

Robert explained that he had just purchased this Rolls Royce, and he inquired, "Have you ever driven in a Rolls Royce?"

Larry replied, "Yes, but never before in the front seat."

Treat Your Customers As If They Have Always Been Driven In Rolls Royces

Never underestimate what your client knows, or what he has experienced. Adjust your expectations. Unless you know for certain, you should assume that he has always ridden in the back seat of a Rolls Royce.

Alex came home and found his wife in bed with another man. He looked at her and said, "This is the end!"

He took a gun out of his pocket and aimed it at his own head. His wife started to laugh.

Alex said, "What are you laughing for? You two are next!" *

Be Careful When Taunting Others ---
You May Be Next

It is often inadvisable to let your guard down because you never know what might happen. Perhaps Alex will realize his error and decide to shoot you first!

---

* My friend Les Weil suggested an alternative. A fellow came home at night and found his wife in bed with his best friend. He took out a gun, shot and killed his friend. His wife said, "If you keep doing this, you will not have any friends left."

This page is intentionally left blank

May I suggest you stop reading this book
and pick up some worthwhile reading like
The Brothers Karamazov by Fyodor Dostoevsky.

Two beggars were sitting side by side on a street in Mexico City. One had a Cross in front of him, the other one a Star of David. Many people walked by and looked at both beggars, but they only put money into the hat of the beggar sitting behind the Cross.

A priest came by, stopped and watched throngs of people giving money to the beggar behind the Cross while none gave to the beggar behind the Star of David.

The priest walked over to the beggar behind the Star of David and said: "My poor fellow, don't you understand? This is a Catholic country. People aren't going to give you money if you sit there with a Star of David in front of you, especially when you're sitting beside a beggar who has a Cross. In fact, they would probably give to him just out of spite."

The beggar behind the Star of David listened to the priest and turned to the beggar with the Cross and said, "Moishe, look who's trying to teach the Levine brothers about marketing!"

Don't Tell The Levine Brothers About Marketing --- Until You Have Heard from Moishe

How many times are we positive that we are right --- and then, when we check into it we find out that our assumptions are completely wrong? Don't tell the Levine brothers about marketing until you ask Moishe a few questions.

A patient told a psychiatrist that he believed that he was a dog. The psychiatrist said, "That is terrible! How long have you felt that you were a dog?"

"Ever since I was a puppy," replied the patient.

Some Of Your Customers Might Have Been Crazy --- Ever Since They Were Puppies

Why should you expect anything from your customers? Business plans are cold, objective, and rational; but business decisions are dynamic and emotional. Don't expect customers to behave rationally. They have probably been crazy ever since they were puppies.

Illustration by Jared Martin

Ever since I was a puppy.

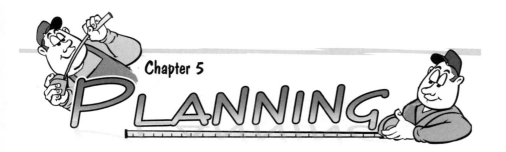

Chapter 5
PLANNING

The goal of planning is to eliminate the urgent, ignore the insignificant and focus on the important. All actions have consequences. Good planning reduces the chance of failure and crystallizes your thoughts. For many important events in life, there is only one chance, and good planning is usually an activity that generates success.

My late partner, Orville Mertz, told me, "If you can't be on time, be early!" He always came early to a meeting, thus eliminating time pressure and giving him time to prepare and review his thoughts. Good planning will often allow you to leave a meeting without thinking, "I wish I had said that."

Monetarily, for every deal there is only one price and that is the final price. All prior terms and conditions have no value. Planning improves your chances that you will benefit from the final price.

No agreement or contract is complete until it is signed. Until that time, almost anything can happen. This is why it is so important to plan and visualize the parties signing the document especially when the deal is important and your expected benefit is large.

Tom wanted a drink. He went into a bar and asked the bartender, "If my dog can talk, will you give me a free drink?"

"Yes," came the reply.

Tom then proceeded to ask his dog the following question, "What is on the top of this building?"

"Ruff, ruff," replied the dog.

In order to cement his case, Tom continued with another question: "Is sandpaper smooth or rough?"

"Ruff, ruff," replied his dog.

Tom looked at the bartender and said, "You owe me a drink!"

"Get out of here!" said the bartender.

After they left the bar the dog turned to Tom and asked, "Did he want me to say that the sandpaper was smooth?"

Many Times You Have One Chance --- And If You Miss, It's Rough On You

For most important events, you have but one chance! Thinking fast is an excellent attribute to develop. Planning ahead is more important. If your dog can speak, tell him exactly what to say. Otherwise, you will be paying for all your drinks and it will be rough on you.

Monks of a certain order were only allowed to say two words every ten years. After ten years a junior monk said, "Bad cold."

Ten more years passed before the junior monk got another chance. He said, "Stomach hurts."

Now ten more years passed at which time he announced, "I quit!"

The head monk replied, "I am not surprised! After all, you have been complaining for thirty years!"

If You Plan Well Enough --- You Will Not Be Surprised At All

Whenever you have something important to do, plan in advance what you are going to say and how you will act. Get to your appointments early. Allocate to planning more time than you think will be required. If you do this, when your junior monk quits after thirty years, you will not be surprised.

A robber walked up to a man on a deserted street corner and asked, "Do you see a policeman?"

The man answered, "No."

"In that case," said the robber, "Stick 'em up."

Even If You Do A Favor --- Be Prepared For A Stickup

Every successful salesman is out there for a stickup. But large decisions only work when the "stickup" is on the surface, a soft or almost nonexistent one. Most successful business people are soft on the outside, and tough within. They are prepared for failure. They use only silent guns.

There was a large clothing store in Manhattan with a sign, "All suits $100."

A man walked in off the street and was greeted by the owner who said, "You are really lucky today, friend, because our price today is not $100 or $90 or even $80. Today, we have one price and it is $75."

The customer looked at the owner and said, "Sir, you are in luck, too, because I have only one price and that is not $75 or even $70. My price is $50."

"Sold," said the owner.

There Are Many Selling Prices --- But Only The Final One Counts

All high priced items — jewelry, houses, businesses — have flexible selling prices. There is only one price for each item, and that is the final selling price on the closing day. All other prices, terms, conditions, etc., are subject to change.

A fellow was seated at a baseball game, and he wanted to get a hot dog. But there were no vendors in the area, so he looked at the little boy next to him and said, "If you get me a frankfurter, I'll give you $2 and you can buy one for yourself."

Shortly, the boy returned, handed the man a dollar, and said, "They only had one frankfurter, and I ate mine, so here is your change!"

Get The Details On Your Contract Correct --- And They Won't Eat Your Frankfurter

No agreement or contract is complete until it is signed. Until that time, almost anything can happen: They can take your money and eat your frankfurter.

It was vacation time and a family went to the airport where a young porter cheerfully assisted with the baggage. The father, who rarely went on trips, asked the porter, "What is an average tip?"

The porter replied, "$25."

The man gave the porter $25 and said, "Young man, you must be doing quite well if the average tip is $25!"

"No," replied the porter. "This is my first average tip!"

They Are Deceptive --- Even When They Get Average Tips

As Thucydides said, "We study the past as a key to the future." Learn about those with whom you will deal by talking to third parties and reading about their backgrounds. Don't ask the porter how much he wants --- or you could be paying the first average tip.

A dad came home from work and scolded his son for not practicing the violin, even after promising to do so. The boy went to his room to practice. The family dog began to howl and continued to howl for twenty minutes while the boy practiced.

The father decided that he had had enough howling, went to the son's room and asked, "Can't you play some piece that the dog doesn't know?"

If You Want Peace And Quiet --- Tell The Kid To Play A New Piece When He Starts To Practice The Violin

All actions have consequences, but unintended consequences are the most common kind. So don't be surprised if the dog howls when your son starts to practice the violin.

Steve Martin wrote the following thought:

Think of a picture of a football and a man.

The man is staring out of a hotel window and he looks depressed.

On the left side of the picture is a football, flying through the air, toward the man. You think about it and you realize that, if he is depressed now, just think how depressed he will be when he gets hit in the head by that football.

Just Because You Are Planning Ahead Does Not Mean You Will Catch The Football

Even with proper planning your customers will surprise you. People are unpredictable and they act on their own beliefs and emotions, which are almost always different from yours. Surprise is one of the excitements of life, and if you accept surprises as inevitable, you will better react when you are suddenly hit in the head by your customer with a football.

Two young men spent a summer on a farm riding horses. At the end of the summer they decided to mark the two horses to tell them apart the following spring. They cut the mane short on one horse and the tail short on the other. When they returned next spring to the horse farm they found that the mane and the tail had grown back.

The first one asked, "Now what are we going to do?"

Replied the other, "You take the black one and I'll take the white one."

Save Time And Effort --- Select The White One The First Time

One key factor in your success will be your ability to simplify complicated issues. A favorite cartoon caption of mine is a businessman on a phone saying, "We have designed this deal specifically so that you would not understand it."

Too many times, through lack of effort and thought, issues that should have been resolved become complicated, unwieldy or insoluble. So, think about things carefully. This will improve your chances of selecting the white horse in the first place.

A young man, badgered by his mother, finally found the woman of his dreams. He told his mom that he planned to bring home the woman and two of her friends, and that he wanted his mother to pick out the one he was madly in love with.

The three women and the young man spent the afternoon with his mom. Later he asked his mom which was the one.

Mom said, "Of course, it is the woman who wore red." He replied, "Yes, but how did you know?"

Mom answered, "It was easy. She was the only one I didn't like."

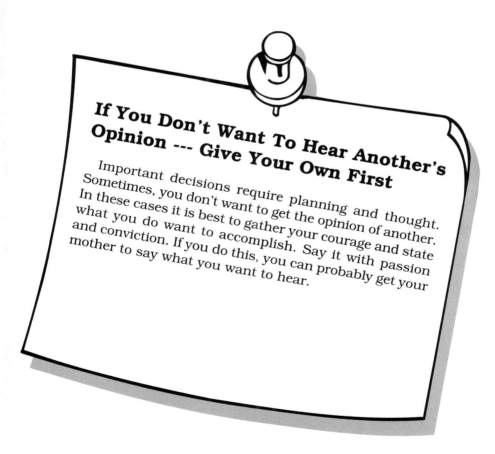

If You Don't Want To Hear Another's Opinion --- Give Your Own First

Important decisions require planning and thought. Sometimes, you don't want to get the opinion of another. In these cases it is best to gather your courage and state what you do want to accomplish. Say it with passion and conviction. If you do this, you can probably get your mother to say what you want to hear.

This page is intentionally left blank

Apparently the author ran out of material.
Perhaps you should try to get your money back.
Good luck!
                                        - Steve

An Italian, an American and Slovak were bragging.

The Italian said, "In Italy, we built a tunnel through a mountain in the Alps that is 50 miles long and a car can travel through this tunnel in 40 minutes."

Then the American bragged, "In the US we have the Sears skyscraper that is 120 stories tall and the elevator reaches the top in 30 seconds."

The Slovak thought for a while, but all he could think of was a man named Pavel in northern Slovakia whose penis is so long that 5 large birds can perch on it when it is erect.

At this point the Italian commented, "Actually our largest tunnel in the Alps is only 35 miles long and it takes almost an hour to travel through it."

Then the American commented that he had exaggerated a bit and that the Sears Tower is only 100 stories tall and it takes about 2 minutes to reach the top."

The Slovak thought for a bit and then said, "You know, Pavel does have a large penis, but actually, even when it is erect, the 5th bird has to lean a little."

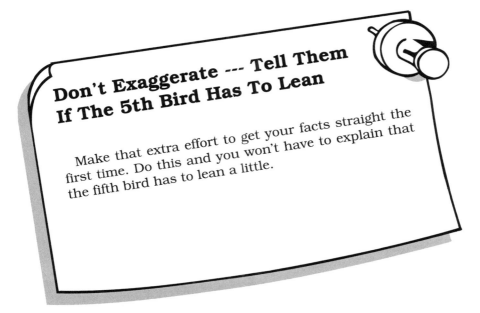

Don't Exaggerate --- Tell Them If The 5th Bird Has To Lean

Make that extra effort to get your facts straight the first time. Do this and you won't have to explain that the fifth bird has to lean a little.

Chapter 6
Decision Making

Whenever we make any decision about a person, there is always a chance that we will be making a mistake, a mistake that we can learn from. After my father would make a mistake, he would say something like "I really made a stupid mistake." My mom would always support him --- "Yes, Ben, that was really stupid!"

Remember the saying that when you make a mistake "your friends will support you, your enemies will fight you and most people won't give a damn."

The most important, and likely the best, decision I ever made was enthusiastically supported by my friends and that was to marry Nancy (although some of them wondered what she saw in me). The success of most major personal decisions such as marriage or business decisions like an acquisition or major investment is verified after the fact. It is affected by luck and factors beyond our control as well as the time, effort and funding that we put into it. As Stephen Leacock said, "I find that the harder I work at it, the luckier I become."

As I grow older, I tend to enter into more negotiations with the thought that my prime goal is that everybody get along. This enhances the chances for success. Many times it is best to defer a decision or to enter a negotiation with the expectation that no decision will be made.

As described earlier in the important joke about the unavailability of roast beef (see page 97) it is often desirable to consider BATNA.* This can help when it is clear that no agreement can be made now because it enables both parties to better understand the obstacles to any agreement and the quality of mutual listening on both sides tends to improve.

It helps to accept the fact that others look at things differently, deal with different rules, and may even be a bit eccentric or crazy (as we may be). When something is important, I try to discern what others are feeling and

---

* Best Alternative To a Negotiated Agreement

thinking which is not necessarily what they are saying. After all, just because someone says something doesn't mean that he means it.

I have found that business leaders often want to solicit your opinion. But a business is not a democracy, and the majority doesn't rule. In large companies it is particularly difficult to understand decisions, since there is often a team of decision makers and the decision making process is less clear. If you want to anticipate a decision properly and get the best advice, ask the person most knowledgeable, usually the boss's assistant or the receptionist.

Decisions are either reversible or irreversible. Irreversible decisions generally require more thought.

For important, long-term decisions, I try to ask myself one question: does it feel right? If I feel comfortable about a decision and not rushed, I can be confident that it is right. So, for important decisions, take your time, get the advice of others and then do what you feel is right. This almost always leads to success.

An absent-minded professor checked out of a hotel and realized he had left his umbrella in his room. He went back to the hotel and was about to enter the room when he heard voices --- a man and a woman were speaking.

The man said, "Whose arms are these?"

And the woman said, "They are mine."

The man continued, "Whose cheeks are these?"

"They are mine," was the answer.

Then the man said, "Whose lips are these?"

And once again, the reply was, "They are mine."

At this point, the professor knocked on the door and said, "When you get to the umbrella, it's mine."

Defend Your Position --- If It's Your Umbrella, Claim It

Deepak Chopra wrote, "If you want attention and appreciation, learn to give attention and appreciation; if you want material affluence, help others to become materially affluent. In fact, the easiest way to get what you want is to help others get what they want." *

To be successful, you must have something to contribute. If you have a good idea, pitch it. If it is your umbrella, claim it.

---

* Deepak Chopra, *The Seven Spiritual Laws of Success*, pg. 31.

A mother saw her son marching in a parade. She remarked to her husband, "Look! There is our son. He is the only one marching in step."

Those Who Love You Will Support You --- Even When You Are Out Of Step

Earlier I mentioned the old saying that "Your friends will support you, your enemies will fight you and most people won't give a damn." Before you accept a compliment as truthful, determine from whom it is coming and the circumstances of his comment. This will enable you to be more realistic and to identify prejudices which otherwise are invisible to you, but obvious to others; and it will prevent you from following blindly those who love or favor you, even when you are out of step.

Illustration by Eric Hungerford

Only our son is in step.

A family went to Miami Beach for a vacation and their small daughter swam too far into the ocean. The family asked the lifeguard to rescue their daughter. But the lifeguard did nothing.

They alerted him again that their daughter might be drowning. Once again the lifeguard did nothing.

So they begged him to tell them why he didn't go out to rescue their daughter. He replied that he could not swim.

Astonished, they asked him how he got the job if he couldn't swim.

The lifeguard replied, "I got the job because I am bilingual." *

Promote Your People According To Their Abilities --- Or Your Lifeguards Won't Be Able To Swim

Select the person who has the most important job skills for each position in your company. If you want to succeed, forget about political correctness. If you don't do what is best for the company and select the most qualified person, the company will suffer. And, of course, if you hire a lifeguard, make sure the lifeguard can swim.

---

* Thanks to Joel Sandberg, my brother-in-law.

A working man had been sick for several days, and the day finally came when he had used up his sick leave. So he called in dead. *

They Are Untrustworthy --- They Call In Dead

---

* This reminds me of Henny Youngman's thought about eulogies:
"My philosophy on eulogies is this: It is better to give than to receive."

The day after the warranty expired, our television broke. We gave it to some men who claimed that they fixed things, but who in fact took it to a mountain hideout where they keep thousands of un-repaired appliances. Then they made popcorn and gathered around the answering machine to listen to messages from my wife. *

Before You Hire A Professional --- Get References On Your References

So! You recognize that you need help, and since you don't have the experience or want to do it yourself, you have decided to seek a specialist for a solution. If it is important, then spend the time to listen to them and evaluate their references. When you talk to that reference, if it is important, ask the first reference for another reference. The second reference is usually more objective and will know whether your prospective professional consultant will fix things or gather around the answering machine listening to recordings of your wife.

* This is a modification of Dave Barry's comment on broken appliances.

Illustration by Jonathan Carnehl

Get references on your references.

On their first date Paul asked Barbara, "Would you like to smoke?"

Barbara answered, "No thanks. What would I tell my Sunday school class?"

Later Paul asked her if she would like to have a drink.

Barbara said, "No thanks. What would I tell my Sunday school class?"

At the end of the date Paul asked if she would like to come up to his apartment and spend the night.

She said, "Yes."

He asked, "What will you tell your Sunday school class?"

Barbara replied, "The same thing I always tell them: 'You don't have to smoke or drink to have a good time.'"

To Have A Good Time ---You Don't Have To Smoke Or Drink

Although we hate to admit it, the fact is that we frequently first make up our minds as to what we want to do and then support it with facts. People are naturally selective in disclosing facts. This is one reason you might hear about a person telling her Sunday school students that they don't have to smoke or drink to have a good time.

An FBI agent was interrogating a suspect in connection with organized crime. He showed the suspect a stack of photographs including one of a notorious mobster. The suspect flipped through the pictures, giving each a routine glance, and said, "I don't know this one, I don't know that one," etc., etc. Finally he came to the infamous mug shot and declared, "And I **definitely** don't know this one."

Check Carefully --- Find Out What The Other Person Really Doesn't Know

Body language, words not spoken, tone of voice and facts not brought out for discussion are just as important as the words that are spoken. So, before you make a decision, try to feel and listen to what is implied.

A telemarketer called one evening and asked for Leah Johansson, who was a newborn baby.

Her mother replied that she was an infant.

"All right," came the reply. "I'll try again later."

All Good Decisions Depend On Good Timing

There is no such thing as a good intrinsic investment or a good intrinsic business idea. All business decisions depend on timing. If you are premature in your timing you will have little chance for success. Better to try again later.

Illustration by Audre Delany

All good decisions depend on good timing.

Nick and Pete were visiting an art museum viewing a painting of three men, all naked and reclining on a beach. All were completely black except that one had a pink penis. Nick and Pete were curious about the meaning of the picture.

Along came a museum curator and when Pete asked for an explanation, the curator informed them that since this was a picture of naked men with no possessions, it was about prejudice against blacks.

Pete and Nick continued looking through the museum when they came upon the museum director. This time Nick described the painting and told about the curator's analysis. The director rejected the curator's explanation and opined that the painting was not about prejudice, but since it depicted three men cavorting naked at the beach, it was a painting about homosexuality.

As Pete and Nick were about to leave the museum, they ran into the artist. Nick told the artist that they admired the beach scene but were confused about its meaning, since the curator had told them it was about prejudice and the director maintained it was about homosexuality.

"Oh no," exclaimed the artist, "The painting is not about prejudice or homosexuality. Actually, the painting depicts three Scottish coal miners and one went home for lunch!" *

Try To Be Like Nick And Pete Who Continued To Delve ---Until They Learned About The Scottish Coal Miners

Often I make the mistake of making judgments too hastily. I have made it a practice of trying not to respond immediately and to inquire and study more before making any major decision. I have found that e-mails in particular seem to call aggressively for an immediate reply. If an e-mail makes me feel uncomfortable, I make a special effort to let it rest for an hour or for a day or two and not allow myself to be pressured to immediately respond. I just try to think of how Nick and Pete continued to inquire until they learned about the Scottish coal miners.

* Thanks to my friend, Bob Bellin

A flight attendant came over to a businessman and asked what he would like to drink. The man answered, "A double martini."

The flight attendant then asked the passenger next to the businessman, who happened to be a clergyman, what he would want to drink. The clergyman answered, "No thank you, I do not believe in drinking alcohol. I would not want to drink alcohol any more than I would want to commit adultery!"

The businessman looked up, handed the drink back to the flight attendant and said, "I didn't know we had a choice!"

Keep Looking For Alternatives --- Perhaps There Is Another Choice

To improve your decision making, it is important to look at all the alternatives so that you can be certain that you are making the right decision. We are all limited by our creativity and our imagination.

One time, when I was doing not so well in creative writing my professor told me, "Mr. Einhorn, you would do better if you extended yourself to Zweihorn." * Although his suggestion did not help my creative writing, it was a creative suggestion.

Why limit yourself to the choices presented to you? There may be another choice.

---

* Einhorn means "one horn" in German. Zweihorn means "two horns" in German.

Two men decided to play Russian Roulette, and the first aimed the revolver and pulled the trigger. No bullet.

Now, the second player aimed the revolver at his head. Once again, no bullet.

The first player tried again, and this time, bang! The bullet went off.

Said the second player, "Do you want to play two out of three?"

Sometimes You Don't Want More Than One Chance

Decide whether a decision is reversible or irreversible. Go slowly on irreversible decisions; go quickly on reversible ones. Sometimes there are important decisions to be made, and you have only one chance.

A wife gave her husband a blue shirt and a red shirt for his birthday. The next day, to please his wife, the man wore the blue shirt. The wife asked, "What's wrong with the red shirt?"

Expect Criticism --- Even If You Wear Their Shirt

No matter how good your intentions, there is always a chance that your decision will be criticized; so there is no reason to be surprised. Just listen; accept the criticism and decide if a reply will be beneficial to you both. Recognize that in some cases the only way not to be criticized is to wear the red shirt under the blue shirt.

I have two boys: David is older, and Daniel is younger. Some years ago they were vying for the only free front seat in our convertible. I recommended that they choose* for the honor. Daniel, said, "I choose to sit in the front!"

See If There Will Be Another Chance --- Even If There Is Only One Front Seat

Sometimes there is an expanding pie with plenty for all and sometimes there is a fixed pie with restricted choices. Let's talk about when there are real limitations and not enough to go around for all. For example, you have to make a choice between two people to determine who gets to do something special: The best choice is usually selecting that person most qualified for the task or who has both the ability and time to do the task properly. Remember that, as a leader, one of your most important responsibilities is to allocate "scarce resources" efficiently and effectively.

In many cases there are two people and only one seat. Sometimes there is a "next time" and two people can each have a turn to sit in the front seat.

---

* Such as eenie, meenie, minie, moe.

New York State Governor Mario Cuomo's wife gave the governor some last-minute advice: "I know you will be giving a speech to a tough group, and these guys know you well. So don't try to be charming, witty or intellectual. Just be yourself."

When You Receive A Suggestion, Accept It Gracefully --- No Reason To Be Offended

Don't allow criticism to offend you. Admittedly, good, honest, well-meaning criticism (or advice) is almost always difficult to accept and also hard to come by. So, when you are criticized, pay particularly close attention and think about it carefully before you reply. No reason to be witty or intellectual about it. Just be yourself.

Sherlock Holmes, the great detective, and his assistant, the devoted and always factual Dr. Watson, went camping. After a couple of hours of sleep Holmes woke up and said to his side-kick, "Watson, look up at the sky and tell me what you see."

"I see millions of stars," said Watson.

"And what does that mean to you?" asked Holmes.

Watson said, "Astronomically, it tells me there are millions of galaxies.

"Astrologically, it tells me that Saturn is in Leo.

"Horologically, it tells me the time is about 3 a.m.

"Theologically, it shows that God is powerful and we are insignificant.

"Meteorologically, it tells me we will have a beautiful day tomorrow."

Then Watson asked, "What does it tell you, Holmes?"

"Watson, you imbecile, someone has stolen our tent."

Even If You Know All About The Universe --- You May Still Lose Your Tent

Don't confuse an avalanche of facts with wisdom. Search for significance and understanding. Search for the "big picture." If you concentrate only on the **facts** and ignore the **big picture**, when your tent is stolen, you will notice only the stars.

Illustration by Dana Borremans

Someone has stolen our tent.

Chapter 7
Control

For me, this has been the most difficult of these introductions to write. I began with the assumption that my goal would be to explain how you could control a situation or convince others to do your bidding, but the more that I thought about it, the clearer it became that the only control we have is over ourselves and our own behavior.

As I thought about control, the words of John Donne kept popping into my mind. He said, "No man is an island, entire of itself; every man is a piece of the continent, a part of the main... Any man's death diminishes me, because I am involved in mankind; and therefore never send to know for whom the bell tolls; it tolls for thee."

John got it right: We are all a "part of the main" and so our actions influence each other. When we communicate with others, we are mutually connected. But "connected" is different from "controlling" and I doubt that in most cases we can or even want to benefit from controlling each other.

I thought of a current example at our company: As I will mention in the chapter on attorneys, clearly the best policy relating to lawsuits is to avoid them. But, once every five years or so our firm seems to get involved in a legal matter. We avoid lawsuits by always agreeing in writing in advance that any dispute is to be resolved by arbitration.

Our firm raises money for others and occasionally a client doesn't want to pay for our services after the money is raised. In our view this happens when the client's ego reaches such heights that he believes that any credit for raising the money belongs to him (our experience is that it has always been a him!).

So we now have a controversy: Should our firm hold out for all of the money due? Should we settle for an amount less than our full fee now? Should we settle just before arbitration begins, or when it starts? Should we go through with the arbitration? Our opponent has a similar array of alternatives.

The question comes down to who now has control over the issue of payment for our services and who will gain control? Clearly, I don't. Attorneys from both sides will claim control and will assure their clients that they have a better than 50/50 chance of winning. Neither we, nor our opponent has control. How should we behave?

My thought is to give up on control and concentrate on my own behavior. I will review the documents, prepare them for the attorney, acknowledge in my own mind that I can't control the result and then monitor the situation as best I can without worrying about a result that many people will have an influence upon and which I don't and can't control.

For me, giving up control provides a sense of relief. I try to look at the situation as a life experience with a curiosity to see how it will end. It is this curiosity which makes the problem into a sort of game. Often the fun comes after you give up trying to take control and allow yourself to become an observer. Life has many surprise endings that can provide us with a great deal of joy.

Joe was a candidate for vice-president of his Union. He was very nervous because he had never run for any office before, and he was worried that he was going to lose. As Joe left his house on election day, his wife comforted him and said, "Don't worry, honey, in our house you will always be vice-president."

Second Place Can Be An Honor --- But Sometimes You Really Want To Be Tied For First

In mathematics, things equal to the same thing are always equal to each other, but in real life, with people and their interrelationships, this may not be the case. Being vice-president may be desirable, but being vice-president at home may not be much better than being second in a singles tennis match!

Benjamin, a young Israeli Talmud student, left Israel for Milwaukee. After a few years his parents came to Milwaukee to visit him.

His mom asked, "Benjamin, where is your beard?"

"Mom," he replied, "In Milwaukee practically no one wears a beard."

Then his dad asked, "But at least you keep the Sabbath?"

"Dad," he replied, "In Milwaukee business is business and almost everyone works on the Sabbath."

His mom asked, "But kosher food you still eat?"

"Mom," he replied, "In Milwaukee it is very hard to keep kosher."

Then there was a pause and his dad asked, "So tell me, Benjamin, are you still circumcised?"

Many Decisions Are Made For Us --- Boys Do Not Vote On Their Circumcisions

Success is very much related to recognizing what is under your control and what is not. In general, you can guide others to react in a certain way, but you cannot control their response. If you want to control other people's behavior, look for where they have no control. For example, you cannot control how Jewish boys will behave when they grow up, but you can make certain that they are circumcised when they are 8 days old.

A 13-year-old boy whose mother was Jewish and whose father was Serbian asked his father, "Am I more Jewish or more Serbian?"

His dad said that he didn't know how to answer and suggested that the boy ask his mother, which he did.

His mom asked why he wanted to know.

The boy replied, "I want to get Johnny's bicycle from him --- and I want to know whether I should negotiate or just take it."

There Is A Part Of Each Of Us That Is Both Serbian And Jewish

All negotiations can be reduced to blends of two simple strategies: fairness and power. These two approaches mark the basis for all negotiations. For the short run, if this is a one-time event and you don't care about your relationship, then **power** is far more effective. If you are looking for a long-term relationship, then seek a negotiation based on **fairness**. When you come down to it, the desired relationship is the basis for whether you should negotiate or take Johnny's bike.

When a pilot told a young boy what he did, the boy exclaimed, "Oooh, a pilot! That must be exciting."
The pilot replied, "Not if I do it right."

Good Business Is Methodical, Professional And Steady --- If You Do Good Business, The Results Will Be Exciting

An entrepreneur has been described as "The Risk Master, always skating on the edge of disaster."* Yes, there is a need for excitement and a need to adjust to change.

Most successful businesses have major components of both **creativity** and **repetition**. Businesses that perform both parts well will have outstanding results. Filing, planning, following up and communicating on a need-to-know basis may be repetitive, but to get exciting financial results they are essential. Running a business may be exciting to the staff but the customers usually expect consistent and repetitive high-quality products and service. Piloting a plane may be exciting to the pilot, but the passengers are seeking a repetitive, dull and timely flight with very little excitement.

---

* From the Draper Fisher Company.

A six year old was having trouble adjusting to first grade. At least twice a week his mother received a note from the teacher describing his latest infraction.

Finally, the mother sat him down and laid it on the line. "I don't want any more notes from your teacher!"

"All right, Mom," the kid replied. "Are you going to tell her or do you want me to?"

If You Want Positive Results --- Be Clear And State Your Thoughts Positively

Negative statements are usually more confusing and produce less successful results than positive ones. For example, if you want to describe the above situation in a complicated, confusing manner you might tell your son that you don't want any more notes and that you probably not prefer that neither he nor you won't have to tell that to the teacher. To gain control, try not to use not, don't, can't, won't or shouldn't. Instead, make it positive and tell the boy to start behaving better and that you want all future notes from the teacher to be complimentary.

As Moe was dying, his best friend, Sam, asked if Moe, after he died, could find out if there was baseball in heaven, and tell Sam before Sam died.

Moe died and kept his promise, returning in spirit that very night, awakening Sam from his sleep and saying, "Sam, after I died earlier today I went to heaven. I have good news and bad news for you. First, let me assure you that there is baseball in heaven, and that is the good news."

He continued, "The bad news is that you pitch on Tuesday."

Identify Clearly What You Want --- Or You May Be Pitching On Tuesday

There are certain decisions that we can make and others that we have no control over. Success requires that we distinguish between them. You can influence whether or not you will pitch on Tuesday, but God will decide if you will pitch in heaven.

Illustration by Kelly Grabko

... you pitch on Tuesday.

A new elementary school was going to raise the American flag for the first time. To make the day special, the Marine Corps color guard was invited to come over and perform the duty.

The day before the ceremony, the school secretary asked the Corps leader whether he was sending Marines who like children. There was a brief pause in the conversation and then the Corps leader replied, "Ma'am, if I tell them to like children, they will like children." *

Always Listen To The Corps Leader

All freedom is relative. Business and social settings have taboos and limitations. In general, if you say things with a smile, use a friendly and gracious tone of voice, and express ideas sympathetically to the listener, your thoughts will be respected. Determine whether the situation is one where you can do as you please or where you are better off doing what pleases another. Sometimes you can do exactly what you want to do; sometimes you can do much of what you want to do --- but you must always do what the Corps leader wants you to do.

---

* An alternative joke which gets to the same thought is this:
    A fellow was promoting the revolution and said, "When the revolution comes you will be able to eat strawberries and cream."
    His friend replied, "I don't like strawberries and cream."
The revolutionary replied, "When the revolution comes you will eat strawberries and cream and you will like it."

There was a problem at the county jail. The safe at the jail was locked and the staff at the jail was unable to open it. The sheriff called in the local locksmith, but he couldn't open it either.

Finally, one of the guards reminded the sheriff that there was a prisoner who was serving time in jail precisely because of his ability to open safes, usually at banks. The prisoner entered the vault, and within 5 minutes opened the safe.

The sheriff asked the prisoner, "How much do we owe you for this?"

The prisoner responded, "Last time I got $500,000."

Don't say "Yes" Before You Find Out How Much They Charged Last Time

It is almost always best to learn up-front what your obligations will be. Do your homework and clarify the cost of a service or product. You will succeed better when you know the value of what is being offered. This may save you from negotiating with a safe cracker who got $500,000 for his last job.

A fellow went to a drug store to buy some condoms, and when he greeted the lady pharmacist, she asked him, "What size do you want?"

He had no idea, so she told him to take off his pants, and she spread her legs and took a measurement. "Size 7," she exclaimed. And he promptly purchased a few dozen size 7 condoms.

A week later his friend went to the pharmacy, and he also asked for some condoms. Using the same advice, he took off his pants, and she spread her legs. "You are a size 8, sir," she said. "How many condoms do you want?"

"None," he answered. "I just came for a fitting."

Qualify Your Customers --- Or They Will Come For A Fitting

Your time is important and continued improvement in the use of your time is the most productive thing you can do for your company. Make a continuous effort to qualify your business prospects and confirm that they have the market and financial resources to become significant customers. If not, you should expect that, at your time and expense, they will come for a fitting.

A girl went up to her grandmother and said, "Grandma, my boyfriend is going to be 21 years old next week, and I would like to give him something he would really like."

The grandma replied, "Forget about what he would like. Give him a tie."

Make It Your Decision If He Should Get A Tie

The first step in making a successful decision about yourself is to think about what you should do. If it is important, keep thinking about it until the answer becomes clear. After hearing the advice of others and considering the alternatives, you, and only you, can determine what is best for you. In this way, it will become your decision whether or not to buy a tie.

Irving was a dressmaker in New York who was hopelessly in debt. He went to his attorney and asked for advice. His attorney advised him, "You are in a tough business, and your suppliers are ruthless. You might as well pretend you are dead."

So, Irving decided to pretend he was dead and arranged a funeral.

At the funeral, along came his friends, his relatives, and his business creditors whom he had not paid.

"Irving," said the first. "You didn't pay my bill, but now you have died and I feel sorry for you and your family."

"You have beaten me," said the second. "I don't forgive you, you bastard. You should not have accepted the last order, but there is nothing I can do."

Another creditor, Harry the cloth maker, looked at the apparently dead body and said, "I should never have sold the goods to you. You beat me out of $100,000. I know you're dead, but I want to have one last satisfaction." At this point, he grabbed a knife out of his pocket and raised it above the deceased.

The corpse arose and said, "Stop! Harry! You, I'll pay!"

All People Are Equal --- But All People Don't Get Equal Results

Faced with the same business challenges, different people get different results. An extra effort can often provide them with an advantage, and thinking problems through and considering the consequences can provide the needed edge --- think of Harry the cloth maker.

Illustration by Carole Pollack

You, I'll pay!

A patient complained to a psychiatrist that he snored so loudly that he woke himself up. He asked the psychiatrist what he should do.

The psychiatrist advised, "When you go to sleep, if you believe you are going to snore, move to another room!"

Be Gracious --- Even If They Ask You To Leave The Room

The key to reacting to lousy advice is to be gracious. Find out the basis for the advice and continue to ask questions until the other person has fully explained his thinking. Many times you will find that the basis for the lousy advice was not so bad at all. At least this way, you will maintain a good relationship with the advisor and you will have a much better chance of having him listen to your advice (even if it is also lousy); and when you give this advice, he will not likely want to move to another room.

A man was told that if he planned to purchase a suit at a certain store, he should offer half price. He walked into the store and selected a suit. The manager greeted him and advised him that the suit would cost $100. The customer offered $50.

The owner cut the price to $50 and the customer decided to continue cutting the price in half by offering $25. This process continued until the customer offered $3 for the suit and the owner, in exasperation, said, "Why don't you just take the suit for free?"

To this the customer replied, "Only if you give me two pairs of trousers."

To Keep Your Pants On --- Distinguish Between Buyers And Lookers

Some buyers are not buyers at all: They are merely lookers. They appear in the marketplace and play the game for fun. They have no intention of buying; they merely want to hear a price. Be careful. They will take the suit from you and also claim two pairs of trousers.

A customer brought a pile of $1 bills into a bank and wrote $100 on the deposit slip. The bank teller counted until he got to $58, and then he threw the bundle down.

"Why did you stop?" asked the customer.

"If it's right this far," said the teller, "It's probably right the whole way!"

When The Other Guy Agrees With You --- He Is Probably Right

When a customer agrees to buy from you, stop negotiating. End the conversation. Get out of there. All he can do is change his mind and decide not to buy. If he buys your product when he hits 58, don't make him count to 100.

Illustration by Rebecca Siahaan

...it's probably right the whole way.

Chuck was leaving a parking space and hit the car in front of him. He stopped, went into reverse, and hit the car behind him. Then he jerked to the left and hit the car in the street that was waiting at a red light.

A policeman observed the incident and came over to the fellow and said, "Young man, I would like to see your license."

"Don't be silly, Officer," said Chuck. "The way I drive, how do you think I could get a license?"

They Drive You Crazy --- Even When They Don't Have A License

You live by your own rules. Other people live by their rules. Your challenge is to use the other fellow's rules to convince him to do what you want him to do.

At a party, Betty saw a friend she hadn't seen for many years. "Bill," she said, "How have things been with you? I understand that your one son has graduated medical school and is now a respected physician, that your other son is now an attorney with a leading law firm, and that your daughter is married in Sacramento with three terrific children, and you stay each winter in Florida."

Bill looked at her and said, "Yes. Then you know."

"Of course," said Betty. "But this is the first time that I am learning the details."

Let Them Do All Your Talking --- And Learn The Details

No one enjoys being pushed, and successful people are the most un-pushable. The more you push, the harder they resist. Therefore, the most direct method to lead them to your goals is indirectly --- with questions, hints and suggestions. Success is allowing the other person to tell your story.

A patient told a psychiatrist that many times he talked to himself.

The psychiatrist said, "That's fine, lots of people talk to themselves. What is wrong with that?"

The patient replied, "You don't know what a pest I can be!"

Be A Pest --- All Successful Salesmen Are Pests

All salesmen are pests. Some are gnats; some are rats; some are lions. For each matter and each negotiation there is an appropriate pest, and it is your job to adjust yourself to be the type of pest that is most effective.

Illustration by Rebecca Siahaan

You don't know what a pest I can be.

A beggar in New York City approached a bank teller. He looked at the teller and said, "Could you loan me $10,000? My only possession in life is this gun."

Listen Carefully To The Guy With The Gun

When you are negotiating and it becomes clear that the other side recognizes the futility of your position, give in quickly and gracefully. Principles are usually worth discussing, sometimes worth fighting for, and rarely worth dying for.

Illustration by Rick Peñaloza

My only possession in life is this gun.

Several theories explain the memory problems of advancing age. One is that the brain is full: It simply has too much data to compute. One solution for older men is to take all the superfluous data swirling around in the brain and download it into the newly-large stomach, where there is plenty of room. This frees the brain to house relevant information. *

Give Your Brain A Rest --- And You Won't Need Your Stomach

When you work too hard and too continuously, your brain overloads. When this happens, tell your brain to take a break and quiet down. Five or ten minutes are usually what it takes for the brain to cool off. Sometimes taking a longer break of fifteen or twenty minutes does an even better job of cleansing. This will enable you to better focus on what is important and you will not need to download trivial data from your brain to your stomach.

* From *Pure Drivel* by Steve Martin.

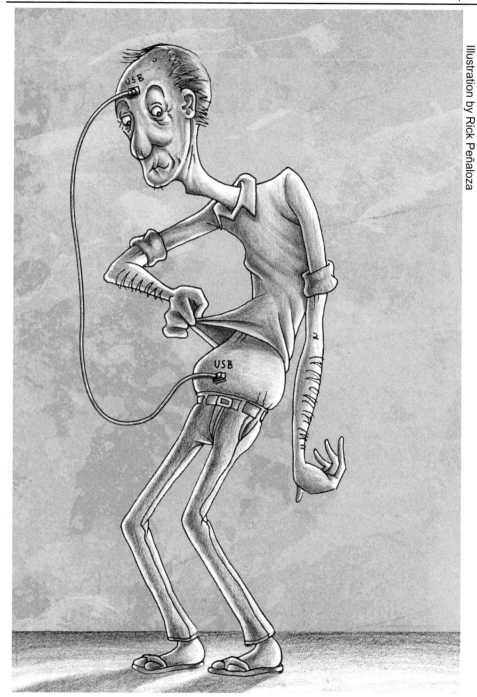

Illustration by Rick Peñaloza

Give your brain a rest, and you won't need your stomach.

Chapter 8
ATTORNEYS
& POLITICIANS

A bar in a small town in England holds a contest to determine the biggest liar in the world. Competitors have five minutes to tell the biggest fib without the aid of props. Politicians and lawyers are barred from entering as they are judged to be professionals.

These are two professions which I believe should be singled out for potential improvement. Of course, this does not apply to my friends who are attorneys or politicians because they recognize that these jokes and recommendations apply only to other attorneys and politicians.

In my view, the fundamental failure of the legal profession is that the vast majority of attorneys have been trained to ignore justice and seek only victory. My suggestion is to select an attorney who has real ability to solve problems rather than define them, who will balance fairness with winning, who can simplify issues rather than make simple things complicated, and, most important, has enough skill to keep you out of law suits which are costly, time consuming and require enormous emotional energy.

Remember that just because you don't agree on an issue doesn't mean that you can't work it out. So get yourself an attorney who knows how to both protect you and get issues resolved.

Many politicians are attorneys and therefore have double handicaps. Most lack the intelligence of good attorneys and also could benefit from improvements in integrity and common sense. They spend our money wastefully and have forgotten how to serve us, their constituents. In their defense, politicians encounter many special interest groups seeking special entitlements and benefits to the detriment of the majority and our country; however, our politicians seem to have no trouble accepting the contributions and following their own self-interest.

Probably, like you the reader, I have many simple, obvious and practical suggestions for politicians which, most certainly, will never be adopted:

(1) Let's make all politicians calculate and fill out their own tax returns in order to guarantee that even an idiot could understand our tax laws.

(2) Let's make a law that, for each new law, politicians must eliminate two existing laws so that we would violate fewer laws each year that we don't even know exist.

(3) Let's limit benefits provided to government employees to what we can afford and let's fund them on a current basis.

(4) Let's concentrate on improving the accountability of the regulators who are entrusted with oversight responsibilities but hide their errors. And let's replace the legislators who ignore their responsibility to oversee the regulators.

It is unfortunate that the majority of politicians and government workers have poor performance records and exhibit limited loyalty to the people who pay their salaries. Most government employees act as if we are responsible to them and they are doing us a favor when they do their jobs rather than that their responsibility is to "serve" the public. Too many work only a portion of their 7 or 8 hour days, never think about their jobs when not working, and dedicate their energies to collecting pensions and other benefits that those of us who are paying their salaries cannot afford.

It is only my exceptional kindness and sensitivity that prevents me from continuing these obviously reasonable and truthful comments about attorneys and politicians.

A businessman had a long-term dispute and decided to see a lawyer to determine the legal aspects of the controversy. After the lawyer heard a one-sided version of the dispute, the lawyer assured the businessman that the case was airtight and asked when they should start the legal proceedings.

"Never," replied the businessman, "I gave you his side of the story."

Before You Make A Decision --- Learn Their Side Of The Story

The most important thing one should know about lawsuits is that one should do almost anything to avoid them. They are costly, time consuming and waste enormous emotional energy. The only sure winners are the attorneys and almost always both clients lose. As Henry Fielding points out in the classic novel, *Tom Jones,* "Juries are always less favorable to us than to other people." Of course, **you are always right,** the problem is that the judge and the jury too often support the other side's version of the story.

Actual testimony in court:

Example #1
Q: Doctor, before you performed the autopsy, did you check for a pulse? A: No.

Q: Did you check for blood pressure? A: No.

Q: Did you check for breathing? A: No.

Q: So, then it is possible that the patient was alive when you began the autopsy? A: No.

Q: How can you be so sure, Doctor?

A: Because his brain was sitting on my desk in a jar.

Q: But could the patient have still been alive, nevertheless?

A: Yes, it is possible that he could have been alive and practicing law somewhere.

Example #2
Q: Now doctor, isn't it true that when a person dies in his sleep, he doesn't know about it until the next morning?

A: Did you actually pass the bar exam?

Select An Attorney Who Understands People --- And Who Should Have Actually Passed The Bar Exam

Many attorneys are so intent on winning that they forget their humanity as they seek more and more facts and separate themselves from human values. Dave Barry has said, "99% of the lawyers give the rest a bad name." I have had several experiences that confirm that Abba Eban was right when he explained that "Attorneys will ultimately do the right thing as soon as they have exhausted all other possibilities."

The Unemployment Compensation Department with the federal government in Washington, DC was reviewing applications for unemployment compensation. The standard form includes the question, "Why did you leave your previous employment?" One applicant, a former U.S. Congressman, responded, "The express wish of 116,000 voters." *

Let's Vote For Candidates Who Are Competent, Have Integrity, Respect Your Rights And Enthusiastically Work For You

I acknowledge that the following comment has nothing to do with the above thought, but I really wanted to put forth a couple of political ideas and could find no better place in this book to put them.

First, I think that congressional term length should be no more than the presidential term limit of two terms. Actually I would prefer one term. This, I believe this would give us more capable and more honest politicians.

Second, I think that its is vitally important to remind ourselves that the fundamental responsibilities of our federal government are (A) to provide for the defense of our nation, and (B) to maintain a fair and level playing field so that each person has an equal opportunity to excel (or fail), and (C) to maintain a stable currency supported by a balanced budget, and (D) to maintain a fair and impartial judiciary.

All other areas where the federal government helps (interferes) including education, health and social security are not its primary responsibilities and, in my view, could better be achieved by the private sector.

Third, I think that the majority of federal employees who have forgotten that they are servants of the people and behave like they are the bosses and policemen of the people should be fired.

---

* Readers Digest March 2000, pg. 67

For a number of years, Harry, a businessman, had been opposed in multiple lawsuits by Joe, an attorney, whose office was only a few blocks from Harry's office. One day Harry went over to talk to Joe and asked Joe's secretary if he could see Joe. The secretary said, "I am sorry to tell you that Joe has died."

A week later Harry went back to Joe's office and, when he saw Joe's secretary, he asked again to see Joe. The secretary said, "I told you last week that Joe had died." Once again Harry left.

Two weeks later, Harry went back and once again asked for Joe. The secretary said, "What is wrong with you? Didn't you hear me tell you that Joe had died?"

Harry said, "Yes. I heard you. I just wanted to hear it again."

People May Say They Want All The News --- But They Really Want Only Good News

Dave Barry wrote that the amoeba, mangoes and many attorneys are all forms of life. He then wrote, "You ask me, how can a mango, which clearly has some value, be related to an attorney?"

My advice to the reader is this: Consider encouraging your children not to be attorneys so that they can avoid a profession where so many contribute less value than a mango.

The mayor of a small city was visited by the mayor of Miami and invited Miami's mayor to visit his home. The mayor of Miami was surprised by the impressive home and furnishings and asked the local mayor how he could afford such an expensive life style.

"See that bridge?" said the mayor, pointing to a distant structure, "I skimmed 5%."

A month later this same small town mayor visited the mayor of Miami and was invited to his new mansion for the evening. The mansion included 50 acres of land, and there were an enormous number of servants available to help during the evening.

The visiting mayor was astounded and asked the Miami mayor the secret of his success.

The conversation went as follows:
"See that bridge?"
"What bridge?"
"100%."

If We Continue Our Excesses --- There Won't Be Any New Bridges

Americans have reached the stage where the majority believe they are entitled: Individuals are entitled to government support for health care and endless hand outs; government workers are entitled to high pay and pensions that make it difficult for government to afford essential services.

This is different from past generations when most Americans wanted the government to leave them alone and a greater number of civil servants acted more diligently to serve their constituents. Too many politicians take what they want, and too many constituencies demand government assistance they don't need.

If we continue in this direction there won't be anything left ---and there certainly won't be any new bridges.

Khrushchev, the Communist leader in 1957, was admiring the annual May Day Parade, and noticed a dozen missiles with huge launchers. He turned to his general behind him and said, "General, those missiles are very impressive!"

Next came thirty large and sturdy tanks. Khrushchev looked again to the general behind him, "General, very impressive!"

Following the tanks were twenty men with blue suits, carrying pens and briefcases. Khrushchev looked at these men and was puzzled. He looked behind him and said, "General, who are those men in the blue suits with the pens and briefcases?"

"Those," said the general, "are attorneys! You have no idea how much damage they can do!"

Beware Of Attorneys --- Beware Of How Much Damage They Can Do

I believe there is a fault in the legal educational system. Many attorneys seem to be trained on how to define problems, rather than solve them. Seek out the majority of gifted attorneys who seek solutions. You have no idea how much damage the others can do.

Illustration by Charles Boston

Beware of how much damage they can do.

A robber in Washington, DC stuck a gun into a man's back and said, "Give me your money."

The man turned around and said, "You can't rob me. I'm a congressman."

The robber said, "OK. Then, give me my money."

Recognize That Most Politicians Forget That They Are Spending Your Money

It has been said that happiness is having a government that lives within its income and without mine.

The basic problem with the vast majority of politicians is that they forget their responsibility and actually believe they are doing you a favor when they spend your money. Until the majority of Americans aggressively attack the waste and pork barreling (and eliminate the "pork" that they might personally benefit from), we will continue to have dysfunctional government spending. There is an old saying that "living well is the best revenge" but if we continue the waste, corruption and deficit spending much longer, no one except the politicians will be living well.

Illustration by Abbey Manalli

Give me my money!

A wealthy man was about to take his wife and three daughters to dinner. He was supporting the daughters through college, and his wife had just decided to go back to school.

His wife said to him, "Let's go to the most expensive restaurant in town to celebrate my return to school."

The man replied, "From now on, we eat at home. Not only do I have you and our three daughters to provide for --- I also have a government to support."

If We Continue To Ask Our Government For More Than We Need --- There Will Be Little Left For Us --- And That Is No Joke

Dave Barry wrote that the folks at the IRS have a terrific sense of humor. Down at headquarters they often pass the time while waiting for their cattle prods to recharge by sending hilarious tax-related jokes to each other, for example: "A lawyer, a doctor, and a priest were marooned on a desert island. So we confiscated their homes."

A father was curious to learn what his son would be like when he grew up. So he put a bible, a $100 bill and a bottle of whiskey on a table in the family den.

He figured that if his son took the bible, he would become a preacher and a man of God.

If his son took the money, he would become a businessman which would improve the economy and help others to support their families.

However, if he took the liquor, then he would become a drunkard and that would be bad.

The son went into the den, looked at the table and, with one hand took a swig of liquor and with the other hand took the money.

The father looked at him and realized he would become a politician.

Expect Politicians To Take Your Money --- And Your Liquor

In 1883 William Sumner wrote an essay titled *The Forgotten Man* which began thus: "The type and formula of most (political) schemes is this: A and B put their heads together to decide what C shall be made to do for D. The radical vice of all these schemes...is that C is not allowed a voice in the matter, and his position, character and interests...are entirely overlooked." As Edwin Fuelner of The Heritage Foundation has commented, "'We the people' of the United States have become the Forgotten Men---forgotten by elected representatives who have been too busy squandering our taxes on self-serving pork to remember us, the people who trusted them to govern."

It has been said that occasionally an innocent is sent to the legislature. But even when an innocent is elected, he usually leaves much of his integrity at the door. There is something about politics that tends to produce in people a feeling of entitlement which leads to abuse of power, dishonesty, and the reckless use of your money. I believe that America will survive best by actively supporting those few who understand whose money they are spending.

This page is intentionally left blank

So stop reading --- and have a beer on me.

A fellow wrote to the Internal Revenue Service: Dear Sirs, I couldn't sleep at all last night, so enclosed is my check for $1,000. I will see if I can sleep tonight. If I can't, I will send you the balance due.

If We Keep Sleeping --- The IRS Will Have All Our Money

It is unfortunate that in the United States the Internal Revenue Service is one of the most efficient branches of the federal government. If the balance of our federal, state and local governments were as efficient as the IRS, there probably would be no deficit, and most of us would gladly pay all monies due because of the high quality of service rendered. The truth is that the quality of our government in general is so low, our politicians have so little insight and distinction, and interest groups strengthen the pieces while they destroy the whole. As long as this continues, the typical American will gladly pay the IRS in full only when he cannot sleep.

A bus full of politicians was speeding down a country road when the bus swerved into a field and crashed into a tree. The farmer who owned the field went over to investigate. Then he dug a hole and buried the politicians and their bus.

A few days later when the sheriff heard about the accident, he drove to the site. He knocked on the farmhouse door and asked where all the politicians had gone. The farmer said he had buried them. "Were they all dead?" the sheriff asked.

"Well, some of them said they weren't," replied the farmer, "but you know how politicians lie."

Be Realistic --- Bury Your Expectations Of Getting A Straight Story From A Politician

Every occupation has its jargon. Politicians use words differently than the rest of us and, for the most part, they don't lie. They just dissemble. Remember that most politicians were trained as attorneys and attorneys are trained to get their way. So, why should you expect anyone trained as an attorney to give you a straight answer?

Cicero said that giving a straight answer is a politician's nightmare. So, when you are dealing with the political process, bury that thought.

Illustration by Charles Boston

They said they weren't dead.

Chapter 9

In 1975 I founded Einhorn Associates, Inc, a business consulting firm. I was the sole employee and so there was no boss. As soon as I hired our first employee, I knew instinctively that I was working for her. I believe that all good bosses work for their staff and make great efforts to adjust to the employees' needs (of course, the staff should make an effort to please the boss).

In his book *Blink*, Malcolm Gladwell tells us that our first impressions and our first guesses are usually correct, and in many cases I would support his conclusion. But often in business, our first impulses as managers are wrong. We all have some bad instincts that require reflection and it is only after reviewing these instincts that the improved thought comes forth. One reason for making slower decisions is that it takes time for the mind to process and often perceptions of self-interest precede thoughts of empathy. *

Whenever you have an immediate thought that might be spoken, consider that it could be wrong and take a moment to think about it. Often, during this brief interim, an improved thought will appear.

The big challenge for every boss is not so much deciding what to do; it is getting members of the team to support each other so that the chances of achieving the desired goals are maximized.

Respect is the key value between employee and employer. There is NO room in business for lack of respect as shown by displays of anger or yelling.

Despite what we read in the newspapers, that business profits must always be maximized, I believe the best bosses balance their short term profit goals with other considerations including: giving employees multiple chances to improve (rather than firing them); accepting needy clients at less than market rates; spending resources on long term disruptive technologies with good potential but high risk; allowing employees with serious personal problems to receive loans or take extra time off. They use company resources to maximize profits as well as support intangible benefits.

In general, bosses that follow their feelings and their values usually make the right long-term decisions.

*Idea courtesy of my friend, Harry Stern

Two brothers were fighting. The mother asked what happened. The first answered, "It all started when Michael hit me back."

Give A Reflected Response --- And You Won't Have To Explain Why You Hit Them Back

How many times do we believe we are explaining a problem and our explanation generates a conclusion opposite from our reasoning? For me, this most often occurs when I put forth an immediate gut reaction that does not take the nuances of the situation into account. All of us have some areas where, for one reason or another, our instincts are wrong, and we must think issues out so that we can overcome our instincts. These are the situations where our gut feelings are emotional and immediately expressing them is not effective. At these times it is best to delay any comment (verbal and particularly e-mail).

For example, my instinct is to not waste time. The problem is that people are more important than time, and so my instinct to get the job done can give short shrift to the personal needs of those with me. This is an area where I now make an extra effort to not react immediately and give more time and respect to the feelings and needs of others. As a result, I now give fewer explanations of how it all started when Michael hit me back.

Beth was looking for a job for several weeks when she found a listing for a job that described her interests and indicated the job would pay a salary commensurate with ability.

Panic stricken, Beth gasped, "I can't live on that."

Earn Your Pay --- By Helping The Company Achieve Its Goals

Yes. Your compensation should be heavily dependent on your contribution, but usually compensation is a balance between your contribution, how the company has performed and the company's attitude toward compensation. It is common for the major compensation issues to be finalized at the end of each year, and too many times there is disappointment.

The trick here is to develop a clear group of identifiable goals and clarify each person's financial expectations. If the outcomes for both the company and yourself meet or exceed expectations, everyone should be satisfied. Recognize that fair compensation is easier to accomplish if your firm is doing well, and much more difficult when expenses exceed revenues or the firm is having a poor year. If the company is doing well and you are making a substantial contribution, you should be able to live on that.

A mother came into the bedroom and told her son, "You must go to school today!"

"But," said the son, "the students don't like me; the teachers don't like me; and even the janitor doesn't like me!"

The mother looked at her son and said, "But you're the principal and you have to go to school!"

Accept Responsibility --- If You Are The Principal, You Must Go To School

Sometimes you don't have a choice: you must act. Step up and acknowledge readily your responsibility: if you are the principal, you must go to school!

Illustration by Sterling White

You have to go to school.

A future prospective employer called to find out about Jerry's work record. He spoke to Jerry's former employer who gave the following report on Jerry: "Jerry did work here. He stopped working here 5 years ago. We are very satisfied."

Just Because Their Work Was Lousy --- Doesn't Mean You Can't Be Satisfied

The current US laws on employment prevent an employer from asking a person's age or marital status. Despite the law, you have a much better chance of mutual long-term success if you voluntarily discuss your status, including your age and marital situation. After all, it is important for both sides to learn as much as possible about each other. You will be spending most of your time at your job, and you want them to know that there is mutual approval and support for your employment.

The laws regarding employment termination make it difficult and potentially dangerous for an employer to give a bad reference, but there remain many ways to indicate that an employee has not performed well. So, do a good job and then your former employer won't report, "He stopped working here years ago and we are very satisfied."

An executive was called for jury duty and asked the judge to excuse him. "We're very busy. I can't afford to be away for an extended period," he said.

"I see," said the judge, "You're one of those businessmen with an exaggerated opinion of yourself. You're convinced that your company just can't function well without you. Is that right?"

"No, your honor. I know they can get along without me. I just don't want them to find out."

If You Are The Boss, Let It Be That They Need You --- Not That You Need You

When you are the boss, you know which parts of the job you do best, and, in fact, there probably are many tasks that you do best or think you do best. So what! If you want to improve your ability to grow the business, cut your ego, show the others confidence and respect that they can do the job. If you accomplish that, you will do your jury duty and allow your staff to show you what they can do.

The boss walked into the office with a duck on his head. One after another, his employees saw this but were too afraid to say anything. Finally, one employee gathered the courage to speak up, "You have a duck on your head. What are you doing? Are you crazy?" he asked.

Then, several other employees gathered their courage and told the boss that he looked ridiculous with a duck on his head. They suggested that he see a psychiatrist. With some reluctance the boss went to the psychiatrist. When the man and duck arrived, the psychiatrist looked at the man and asked what is wrong?

The duck answered, "Get this guy off my ass."

If You Are The Boss --- Don't Duck That Fact

If you are the boss, you want your people to like you and be your friends. However, no matter how nice and considerate you are and no matter how hard you try, you are still the boss. Therefore, it is proper to maintain some distance between yourself and your subordinates. It is best to accept the fact that there will be times when your staff feels that they would really like you to get off their ass.

Illustration by Daniel R. Williams

Get this guy off my ass!

President Carter once gave his Secret Service driver directions to Plains, Georgia, but the driver continually made wrong turns. Carter would re-explain the route, but after a few tries, he added, "Or we could go where you want to go."

Success Depends On Helping The Boss To Go Where The Boss Wants To Go

Before your trip, take a few minutes and look up where you are going. Then, think about how you are going to get there. Don't let your ego or laziness prevent you from mapping your trip. This will save you time and anxiety during the trip. It is nice to get directions --- but it is even better to have a map (or GPS), so that you actually know where you are going. Most important, if you have a map and review it, without anxiety you will get to where you want to go --- or if you are traveling with the boss, you will go where the boss wants to go, on your first try.

A manager was about to hire a new employee, and he decided to call the previous employer for a reference.

"Was he a steady worker?" asked the prospective new boss.

The past employer replied, "Was he steady? Why, he was motionless!"

It Is Your Responsibility To Either Mentor Or Fire A Problem Employee --- So You Have The Type Of Steady Worker You Want

Insubordination, apparent lack of integrity and lack of effort are the three most common serious problems that I have run into with employees.

When there is a serious problem with an employee you naturally want to discuss the problem with the employee and those who might provide reasonable input. After these discussions, the question to be asked is: Does the employee have a reasonable chance of correcting the problem? If the answer to the question is NO, then don't be motionless, make a change and hire a steady worker.

Personnel decisions should be made promptly. If you are not sure about an employee's performance, it is probably not satisfactory. Then the question becomes, is it worth your time and the company's time to try to rectify the problem --- or should there be a change in personnel?

The president of a high tech company arrived early one morning at the office and answered the phone. When he asked how he could help, the caller inquired what his job was.

"I'm the president," he replied.

"That's all right. I will call back later. I need to talk to someone who knows something."

Just Because You Are The President --- Doesn't Mean You Know Something

When you contact a business, greet the receptionist as if the receptionist were the president of the company. The person who greets you quite likely knows more about the day-to-day workings of the company than the president does, and a really skilled president promotes this knowledge and interest.

Great leaders know what they do best, and the best leaders understand their limitations. They know and use to advantage their ability to find and select those employees who most likely will succeed at a given task or project. They think about this sort of thing and make sure that at their company the customer will talk to an employee who does know something.

Isaac owned a small ranch in Texas.

The Texas Hourly Wage Department, believing that Isaac was not paying proper wages to his help, sent an agent to interview him. "I need a list of your employees and how much you pay them," demanded the agent.

"Well," replied Isaac, "There's my ranch hand who's been with me for 3 years. I pay him $600 a week plus free room and board.

"The cook has been here for 18 months, and I pay her $500 per week plus free room and board.

"Then there's the half-wit who works here about 18 hours every day and does about 90% of all the work. He makes $10 per week, and I buy him a bottle of bourbon every Saturday night."

"That's the guy I want to talk to --- the half-wit," said the agent.

"That would be me," replied Isaac.

When You Need Help --- Don't Count On The Texas Hourly Wage Department

If it is your company and you are losing money or you are participating in a start-up, the hours are usually long and the pay is short. Lots of cash will flow out and rarely will cash come your way. When business is difficult it will likely take much more time and twice the money to get the results reversed so that your cash flow will be positive. When you have a cash flow problem, don't expect sympathy from the Texas Hourly Wage Department.

A rich but cheap entrepreneur had developed a large mining property extending several hundred miles employing several thousand people. The owner took out millions of dollars each year, but paid the employees very little.

One day he went for a ride in his private plane to survey his property, and in a generous gesture he dropped $20 out of the window and said, "Here, this will please one of my employees."

Still surveying the property, he dropped $40 out of the window and said, "Here, I will please another employee." When the pilot heard this, he shouted, "Why don't you jump out yourself and please them all."

Be Generous --- And They Won't Want You To Jump

On the one hand an entrepreneur is commonly admired for vision, energy, risk taking and determination. Another important trait for an entrepreneur is generosity with his employees. After all, the entrepreneur can't succeed without the contributions of key employees. Don't fall into the trap of allowing your ego to believe you deserve an excess of the benefits. Define stiff goals for your key employees and, for those that excel, when there is a choice, pay them the highest amount that you might be considering. If you are generous here, you should expect big future results. Excellent compensation is a big step toward pleasing them all.

Illustration by Ryan Carter

...Please them all.

Chapter 10
WORRY & GUILT

There is a difference between me and you:
If you say you've got troubles as big as my own,
I'm forced to admit that it is true;
But consider the fact that mine happen to me,
While yours merely happen to you.**

One million years from now no one will remember anything that you ever did or what anyone else who is living ever did; and, if somehow they should find out what you or anyone else who is now living did, they would not care very much. So, why worry?

Milton Berle, the great comedian, made a serious comment on worry when he said, "Worry is the interest we pay on trouble before it is due."

Why is it that we concentrate on our problems and spend so much time worrying about issues that we have no control over or things that are not important? Perhaps it is because we are unable to recognize those things that we have no control over and because there is a natural tendency for all of us to try to perfect the meaningless. It is only effective to focus on those things you can change, since if you can't change them, worrying won't help. So, you might as well concentrate on addressing major opportunities and potential rewards.

Since all we can control are our own actions and behaviors, when I have a problem, I try to remind myself that I am doing my best, that I should be enjoying the journey of life and, most importantly, that I am a good person. Therefore, no reason to worry.

I believe that if you picture yourself as caring and gracious, both on the outside and inside, (that is, your face to the world and your picture of yourself) your worries will tend to disappear and your days will be full of sunshine.

Shakespeare wrote that "Those whose guilt within their bosom lies,

* Herbert Prochnow

235

imagine every eye beholds their blame." It is this fear which for most of us is derived from our parents and religion, that teaches us the difference between right and wrong and provides guideposts for our behavior.

In business, it is guilt that often guides us to do the right thing according to our values because if we do the right thing, we don't feel guilty.

I have learned that when I make a mistake, for irrational reasons I tend to feel guilty, whether it was intentional or not. At this point, it usually takes two or three days to completely wash the guilt of making this mistake out of my system. With this time passing, I try to identify what I have learned from the mistake, and then go forward, completely concentrating on other matters --- like doing new productive things and enjoying myself.

During services, the pastor, emphasizing the importance of not worrying, assured the congregation that "ninety percent of the time, the things we worry about never happen."

"So," commented a parishioner, "Worrying works!"

Worrying Works, But So Does Not Worrying --- And Not Worrying Usually Makes Much More Sense

Why is it that we spend so much time worrying about problems and areas where we have not succeeded? If you have read this far in my book, then clearly you are not a failure. Yet, quite likely you worry about things too much.

Since worrying is not productive, you really want to concentrate on those areas that offer your greatest opportunities and potential for success. Your efforts toward problem solving are the better way to go.

So think about those things that you can change because if you can't change them, worrying won't help.

Many years ago, when I was in the paint business, we wanted to call another company to find out if a Mr. Silverman worked there. A secretary named Stephanie was given the assignment. She called the company, and asked for Mr. Silverman.

She was connected to Mr. Silverman, who asked, "Who is calling?"

"This is Stephanie," said our inexperienced secretary.

He yelled, "Stephanie, I have told you never to call on Tuesday! My wife is here on Tuesday, and she is here now! Goodbye!"

Your Customers Might Be Full Of Guilt --- Don't Call Them On Tuesdays

Guilt runs deep. Those annoyed with themselves yell the loudest. At the highest levels of business, yelling is rare: It reflects confusion, surprise, lack of self-control or guilt. To the receiver, it reflects weakness or attempted intimidation. However, yelling can be very beneficial, especially if practiced in a locked bathroom or solitary automobile. It can also be helpful if Stephanie calls on Tuesday.

The parents were concerned because their 8-year-old son had never spoken. One day, the silent 8-year-old was eating oatmeal with his parents and to their great astonishment he suddenly said, "Could you pass the sugar for my cereal?"

The parents were excited, and they asked the child why he had not spoken for the first 8 years.

The boy replied, "Until now the service has been very good."

If You Didn't Hear Any Complaints --- The Service May Be Good

How often do we worry about a customer or people problem when there is none? We believe that we have erred and we act to correct the problem only to find out there is no problem. If we suspect a problem, without verification, it is often best just to have a friendly chat or phone call. You can often tell from the tenor of their reaction whether there is real dissatisfaction and whether or not the service has been very good.

There was a terrible fire, and fire engines from several fire departments came to assist with no success. Finally, the Big Green fire department came to the fire, but instead of stopping outside the fire, the Big Green fire engine drove right into the center of the fire and, miraculously, the firefighters inside were not hurt as they successfully put out the fire.

The mayor was so pleased with the bravery of the Big Green fire department that he offered them a reward of $50,000. Then he asked what they would do with the money.

The Big Green fire chief thanked the mayor and said, "Well, the first thing we will do with the money is fix the brakes on the fire truck."

Great Things Can Happen --- Even If You Don't Fix The Brakes

Most folks are afraid to make a decision because they are afraid to make a mistake. So, instead of thinking for themselves, deciding what to do, and doing it, they wait until they get a directive from another. In this way they avoid being responsible for making a mistake. These people should be encouraged to make their own decisions which will increase their self-confidence. Also they will accomplish more, make fewer mistakes and sometimes, even if they make a mistake, they can get as lucky as the Big Green fire department was when its truck lost its brakes.

While driving her daughter to school, a mother drove through a red light and said, "Oh, no, I just went through a red light."

The daughter comforted her and said, "I guess it is all right. The police car behind us did the same thing."

Just Because You Made A Mistake Doesn't Mean You Were Wrong

Mistakes don't necessarily cause problems. Making a mistake (unintentionally going through the red light) often has no consequences or merely minimal consequences. But having a problem (the policeman notices you or you hit another car) usually requires time, energy and expense.

In business there are many "red lights," both real and artificial. Some are significant, like serious lapses in personal behavior or absence of basic required knowledge. Many "problems" are not really problems at all, they are just unjustified rules based on tradition, politics or emotion. Your job is to distinguish between these and act accordingly.

A visitor overcame her fears and joined a trail ride down the Grand Canyon. As she descended she tried to ignore the pebbles and small rocks that, loosened by the mule's hooves, fell to the valley floor. Then she overheard one trail guide remark to the other, while nodding at her mule, "I thought they'd retired Old Stumblefoot."

Develop More Inner Confidence --- And You Won't Worry About Old Stumblefoot

Others can strengthen or try to weaken your confidence, but meaningful confidence comes from within. Try to develop a view of the world, one which clearly identifies your values, your dreams and your goals and then, when you have a problem insert that problem into your value system and see where it fits. This will make it easier for you to decide what to do and justify your confidence that you are doing the right thing. Your confidence will increase and you won't worry about Old Stumblefoot.

Illustration by Lauren Rubin

I thought they'd retired Old Stumblefoot.

A fisherman went into a bait shop and asked for 50 cents worth of worms, "And, by the way," he asked, "How many worms do I get for 50 cents?"

Came the reply, "Don't worry, son, I'll do right by you. Life's too short to be counting worms."

Think About What Is Important --- And You Will Never Have To Count Worms

When it comes to concern about what things cost, I find that it is helpful to decide in my mind that there is some amount of money, say $100, that even, if I think I am not getting a good value, I won't allow it to bother me. This eliminates many potential petty mental grievances and helps me to not "sweat the small stuff."

Each person decides for themselves what is their MTA (Monetary Threshold of Annoyance). For some, it is $10 for some it is $10,000. The important thing is to decide what that number is for you.

Many folks you work with will practice frugality to the detriment of their personal success. They pay attention to the pennies and ignore the dollars. They have firm opinions on copy machine costs and no opinion on the company's long-term strategy. They will not bring success to your company.

It has been said that misers are terrible to live with, but they make great ancestors. How often do we become concerned about something and, after lots of worry, determine that it was not important. We worry about losing things that are not important. Learn to give up on the small stuff. Life is too short to be counting worms.

At graduation from high school the principal congratulated the graduates for their achievements and commented that this was not the end of their relationship with the school. In fact, he suggested that they get together in this very auditorium 25 years from today.

After a moment of silence, one voice piped up, "What time?"

Good Timing Comes More From Experience Than From Any Other Factor

George Carlin said it well, "Have you ever noticed that anybody going slower than you is an idiot and anyone going faster than you is a maniac?"

Timing is always a challenge. If you go too fast, you annoy your customers; if you go too slowly, you can miss your chance. If you are young and your timing seems bad, don't worry about it. Good timing comes from experience and, with 25 years of experience, you will have a better chance to get it right.

A 6-year-old boy came to his father and mother and told them that he was about to get married to the girl next door, who was also 6.

"Where will you live?" asked his father.

"At her house. She has an extra room."

"What about money?" asked his mother.

"She has an allowance of 25 cents. I get 50 cents. Our needs are modest," replied their son.

"What about children?" asked the mother.

Replied the boy, "Bite your tongue! So far we've been lucky."

Bite Your Tongue --- While You Work To Distinguish Between Apparent And Real Problems

Some problems are apparent. Some problems are real. If another thinks the problem is real, it is real --- even if it is really only apparent. Fortunately, 6-year-olds usually don't get married or have children, and yet, married folks can act like 6-year-olds. So, bite your tongue.

Tony, who was 4 years old, was staying with his grandmother for a few days. After playing outside with his friends, he came into the house and asked his grandmother, "What is it called when two people are sleeping in the same room and one is on top of the other?"

Grandmother was a bit taken aback, but decided to tell him the truth, and said, "It's called sexual intercourse, darling."

Tony just said, "Oh, OK" and went back outside to play with the other kids.

A few minutes later he came back in and yelled, "Grandma, it is not called sexual intercourse! It's called Bunk Beds! And Jimmy's mom wants to talk to you!"

Freud Was Partially Right --- But All Issues Do Not Revolve Around Sex

Sometimes we worry excessively about non-issues and we create our own problems: that is, we imagine problems when no problems exist. To some extent we can blame this on our language because the English language is so rich with multiple meanings that the language itself can lead to misunderstandings. This is one reason why so many of us are thinking about sex when we should be thinking about bunk beds.

A writer was sitting in a plane next to the window with a 280-pound football player called Bubba in the aisle seat. The writer wanted to go to the bathroom because he was feeling nauseated. He was about to leave his seat when he noticed Bubba was sleeping. Since Bubba had just lost his last game and was in a bad mood, the writer decided not to trouble Bubba and to let him sleep. A few minutes later the writer got sick and vomited all over Bubba's lap.

When Bubba woke up, the writer asked without missing a beat, "Feeling better, Bubba?"

Ask Questions --- And You Will Find Out If Bubba Is Feeling Better

Almost always, when we hesitate to do the right thing for ourselves because we are intimidated, the result is undesirable for both parties. There is a balance between thinking about how you can help and allowing yourself to be taken advantage of due to insecurity or guilt. If you think about a problem for a minute or two, often you will be able to decide what is right for that circumstance and make a decisive move. So, if you don't feel well, wake up Bubba, use the bathroom, and you won't have to ask Bubba if he is feeling better.

Illustration by Sterling White

Feeling better Bubba?

Chapter 11
INTEGRITY

Integrity is doing the **right thing** for the right reasons in the right manner. Each of us has the responsibility to act honestly and do what is right in accordance with our **fundamental beliefs** of what is right and wrong. Although theoretically ethical considerations are often black and white or right and wrong; in negotiation and diplomatic matters, solutions **are by their nature ambiguous.**

When we are faced with a conflict between two values, each of which has some virtue, we should choose that path that is **most effective for both sides**. To act with integrity requires a combination of **Information, Skill and Values:**

> **Information** relates to the search for the knowledge necessary to make a decision;
>
> **Skill** relates to integrating the process in putting the idea properly into action; and
>
> **Values** are determined by a set of beliefs that distinguishes right from wrong.

In general, the best that each of us can accomplish in connection with ethical decisions is to do what feels right. Fundamentally, in ethical decisions, the heart is usually a better guide than the mind.

A boy about 9-years-old knocked on my door. He said that something of his had found its way into my garage and he wanted it back. I noticed two additions to the garage: a baseball and a baseball-sized hole in the garage window. "How do you suppose this ball got in here?" I asked.

The boy looked at the ball and the window and said, "I must have thrown it right through that hole."

It Is Not Their Fault --- They Threw It Right Through The Hole

When someone makes a mistake, the most common explanation you will hear is NMF (Not My Fault), NMP (Not My Problem) and NMJ (Not My Job). Therefore, be prepared to hear NMF, NMP and NMJ.

I believe that the best policy for all to adopt is "If you touch it, it's yours." That is, everyone associated with a project is responsible for its success. So you might as well tell the boy next door that he was correct that the ball did go through the hole, but that the window didn't have a hole before he threw the ball.

Illustration by Kelly Grabko

I must have thrown it right through the hole.

Ole and Olga were eating dinner and the doorbell rang. They both went to see who was there. It turned out to be a masked criminal who said to Olga, "I'm going to kill you, but first tell me your name."

Olga said, "Olga."

The criminal said, "I can't kill you. Olga is my mother's name and I can't kill anyone with my mother's name."

Then he turned to Ole and asked what his name was.

Ole said, "My name is Ole, but all my friends call me Olga."

If Your Life is Threatened --- Just Call Yourself "Olga"

There are rare instances when it is a mistake to be truthful. For example, if you have confidential information that you are not allowed to reveal (in which case you should usually say that whatever you know is confidential), or when your comment could seriously harm an innocent person, or if your life is in danger. If a gun is pointed at your head, it makes good sense to become "Olga."

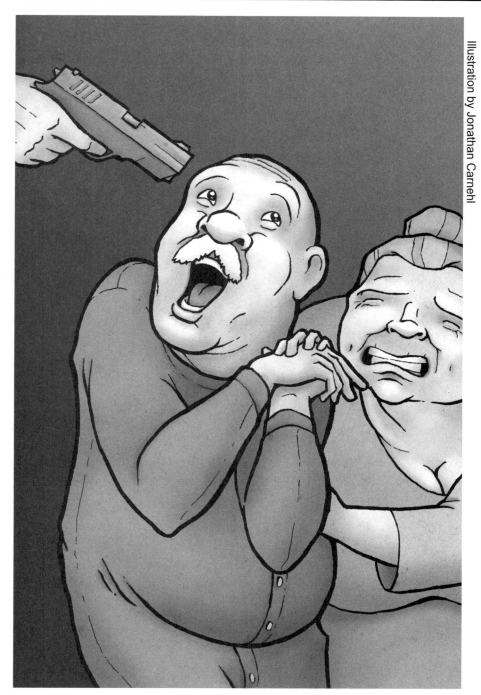

Illustration by Jonathan Carnehl

My friends call me Olga.

In a business ethics class at the University of North Texas, the class was discussing sexual harassment in the workplace.

Turning to a female student, the male professor asked, "What could the consequences be if I offered you an A or a B in this class in return for a relationship?"

The student replied matter-of-factly, "To have a relationship with you, I would want at least an A."

When It Comes To Ethics ---
Everyone Expects An A

For ethical questions it is important to realize that almost everyone believes their ethics are above average. Almost everyone claims to have high integrity, to show high respect, to deserve trust and, of course, to have excellent morals. This is why when you are working with others, learn how they define their values (especially respect, trust and integrity). Remember that when others grade their own values, virtually everyone believes she deserves an A.

Max and Abe were walking down the street. Max noticed some dog crap on the sidewalk. He said to Abe, "That looks like dog crap!"

He then bent down so that he could smell it, and said, "It sure smells like dog crap!"

Finally, just to be sure, he tasted a bit of it, spit it out, and said, "It is dog crap!"

Abe looked at Max and said, "Well, at least you didn't step in it!"

If It's A Crappy Situation --- Get Out Before You Step In It.

Your actions should not even have the appearance of impropriety. Whenever you feel uncomfortable about a business situation, whether you believe that it might be dirty, perhaps unethical or steeped in potential conflict of interest, get out --- before you step in it.

After a fishing trip an ardent fisherman bragged to his friend that he had caught a 20-pound fish.

"Were there any witnesses?" asked his friend.

"Of course," came the reply. "Otherwise the fish would have weighed 30 pounds."

Be Sure There Is A Witness --- Or The Fish Will Weigh 30 Pounds

E-mails and telephones are nice. But if something is important, you want to be there. Being there is the best way to learn and enhance your chance of success, especially when some important open issues need to be resolved. It is easy to be lazy and talk over the phone, but then the fish will probably weigh 30 pounds.

Illustration by Mara Natkin

Be sure there is a witness.

In 1950 in Italy, five years after World War II ended, a man confessed to his priest that during World War II he had hidden a refugee in his attic.

"Well," said the priest. "That is not a sin."

"But," the man admitted, "I made him pay rent."

"Well, that was not nice...but you did put yourself at risk," commented the priest.

"One more question," asked the man. "Do I have to tell him the war is over?'"

Integrity Requires Complete Transparency --- So Tell Them That The War Is Over

There are many times when it is desirable to be intentionally vague: For example, when a matter is highly confidential, or when telling a person something will harm them considerably more than it will help them, or when you feel like criticizing someone for something that is not important. But there are other times when the issue is a matter of significance, or what an attorney might call "material," and there, only complete disclosure is appropriate. It is often unnecessary to report about a skirmish, but unless you are willing to accept disastrous consequences, you must tell them when the war is over.

Illustration by Ryan Carter

Do I have to tell him the war is over?

A Vermont native inherited some property including several buildings and put one of the buildings up for sale.

A prospect looked at it and said, "I'm interested. Are you flexible on the price?"

"Yes," the Vermonter replied, "I could go up."

Be Careful When Negotiating To Buy Something --- The Selling Price Might Go Up

Much of business is trying to determine what is fair. One time, I was working on a business dispute and the buyer offered to split the difference which was about $500,000 and commented that that would be fair. The seller replied, "Fair for you --- but not fair for me." So, when you are the buyer and negotiating and asking for fairness, remember that for the other fellow, fair might mean UP.

Justin and Aaron tried hard but could never please their father. Whatever they did seemed wrong to him and they were constantly criticized. Finally, the father became so frustrated with them that he decided to send the boys to the rabbi.

Justin went to the rabbi's office and the rabbi asked, "Where is God?" Justin was unable to answer so the rabbi said, "Think about it and I will come back in a half-hour." A half-hour later the rabbi returned and repeated, "Where is God?" Once again Justin did not respond and the rabbi said that the boy should think about it.

This process repeated for a couple of hours at which point Justin, snuck out of the rabbi's office and ran home.

There he found Aaron and said, "Guess what? I am in trouble. They have lost God and they think I know where he is!"

There Are Some People You Will Not Be Able To Please --- And Will Criticize You For Not Doing The Impossible

The fact is that those people who don't like or respect you will blame or criticize you regardless of your actions; and, from their perspective, if God is missing, it will be your fault.

This page is intentionally left blank

So since you are not doing anything productive,
this is an excellent moment for you to think of
10 friends who might want to purchase this book
at retail.

A man bought a parrot. The parrot continually cursed. The man decided to teach the parrot a lesson and warned the parrot to watch his words or be punished. When the parrot continued to curse, the man put him in the freezer for 5 minutes. When the parrot was released he asked, "I know what I did; but what did the chicken do?"

Behave --- So That You Don't Get Treated Like A Chicken

Of course, you recognize that the man saw the issues differently: he put the parrot in the freezer for bad speaking and the chicken in the freezer for good eating. Isn't it interesting that the chicken, which did nothing to irritate the man, got the worst of the punishments, while the parrot escaped after 5 minutes? Is that fair? No, life is not fair, but cursing won't change it.

A nurse stopped a doctor who was about to start writing with a thermometer, and said, "Doctor, you are writing with a thermometer!"

The doctor looked down, saw the thermometer, became annoyed, and said, "Some asshole has my pen!"

Don't Be Careless --- Or Some Asshole Might Have Your Pen

Sometimes you think you are accomplishing one thing, when actually you are doing something quite different. Keep your mind on the matter at hand, or some asshole might take your pen.

Some asshole has my pen.

Chapter 12

SUCCESS

For the first 10 years of my business life I worked for the family business, Adelphi Paint and Color Works, Inc. The harder I worked, the worse we did. The company was profitable when I joined, but after 10 years of effort, we were close to bankruptcy. My dad allowed me to sell the business. We paid off our debts, and I had a fresh start. Naturally, I blamed myself and looked at my own career as one with FAILURE written all over it.

During the past 30 plus years, I have enjoyed some successes (and some notable failures). For two years I tried to work with two junior partners and failed; for years I tried unsuccessfully to end a business dispute that had lasted for over 10 years; my consulting efforts in the Czech Republic failed after 5 years. I wish it could be said that for each of these failures I learned how to prevent future failures --- but the fact is there are so many ways to fail that this is not the case.

Much success has to do with good fortune: I entered the merger and acquisition business early and it grew into a large industry; our firm has talented and loyal employees; we represent many unique firms which make important contributions to our society; and we have the opportunity to work with some exceptional people. Success comes along with good luck, hard work, good people and really liking what you do. I attribute most of my own success to two personal traits which I have continually made efforts to strengthen: patience and persistence.

My dad expressed this idea so well when he explained why his marriage to my mom was successful. His words were, "Mom and I have been married for 60 years. If you want to know why my marriage was successful, it really is simple and it is a lesson that I can share with you. Just remember, in a marriage the first 59 years are the hardest."

I know that many times one thinks of success in terms of making money, and that certainly is a pleasure. But as has often been said, "Success is the journey," and there is a time during that journey that you feel that you have accomplished something. In investment banking these highlights are things like getting two people who have been feuding for a long time to appreciate each other; getting to that point in the deal where the major obstacles have been overcome and you are confident that the deal will close. There is a unique sense of personal satisfaction to those times in your life when you have reached the top of the mountain and you know that the walk down will be sheer enjoyment.

In this book I have already mentioned certain measures of success. Here are a few more thoughts.

Success comes from having a great spouse; helping your children to grow up into fine adults and being proud of them; understanding others better and encouraging them to feel good about themselves; distinguishing right from wrong and doing the right.

At the end of this book I have included an outline of my current values, goals and dreams. These are ideas that I have developed over many years and have updated regularly. I do this because I believe that if my actions are guided by my values, and if I pursue my goals with good spirit, I will achieve my dreams and have led a successful life.

And finally, success comes from enjoying a good joke and laughing.

John picked up a $500 a night prostitute and took her to a hotel. As she undressed, he noticed that she was wearing a Star of David.

He asked, "Are you Jewish?"

She said "Yes."

He commented, "So am I."

She replied, "OK. Since you are Jewish, the price will be only $300. But let me tell you this --- there is no profit in it for me." *

When They Tell You There Is No Profit In It For Them --- Be Especially Careful

When you are presented with a deal that seems too good to be true, ask yourself, why am I so lucky to be given this opportunity? More than likely, the deal is very good and the profits are real and large, but they go to the other side.

---

* The story reveals a bit about political correctness. Since I am Jewish, I can tell this joke. If I were not Jewish, the joke would likely be considered anti-Semitic. Same goes for black jokes. Recognize when you are not the right person to tell the joke --- or modify it so that it becomes appropriate. Otherwise there may be personal reparations to be paid.

A truck driver was driving in a long line of tractor-trailers when a police officer pulled him over for speeding. Annoyed that he was the only one caught, he asked, "Out of all these trucks that were going just as fast as I was, why did you pull me over?"

"Have you ever gone fishing?" The officer asked.

"Yes," came the reply.

"Well, have you ever caught all the fish in the lake?"

Don't Be Surprised If You Are Chosen --- No One Catches All The Fish In The Lake

Life is not fair. Every now and then you will be that unlucky truck driver. There are usually two factors to consider: luck and fairness, because luck still determines many results and people look at fairness differently.

You will become more successful by realizing that other people are almost always fair according to their standards and that their standards are different from yours. I believe that each of us tries to be fair according to his own standards. So don't expect others to be fair according to your standards. Most are not out to catch all of the fish in the lake.

Illustration by Heidi Schwartz

All the fish in the lake.

Evan went to college and wrote his father a letter, "Dear Dad, today I tried out for a play and got the part. I play a man who has been married for 20 years."

The father wrote back, "Dear Evan, Congratulations! Keep up the hard work and next time you will get a speaking part."

You Still Can Contribute --- Even If You Don't Have A Speaking Part

I have found that, most of the time, others are not impressed with your success. Telling about your success will not make you more successful. The most successful people I have met do not have large speaking parts: they have large listening parts.

As part of an English assignment in seventh grade one girl wrote, "If I could have one wish, I'd choose world peace. And if somebody has already chosen that, I'd wish for a boyfriend."

If You Are Not So Lucky --- You May End Up With A Boyfriend

When I identify a goal, I often try to use the technique with the acronym SMART (Specific, Measurable, Attainable, Results Oriented, Time Bound). This reminds me of the specific components which are usually necessary to achieve any goal.

When identifying your goals, consider that one of the most important components is the determination of whether your goal is a fantasy or is truly attainable. Maybe you can't create world peace --- but, with diligent effort, you should be able to get a boyfriend.

There is a story about a father whose daughter was drawing a picture and the father said, "What are you drawing a picture of?"

"This is going to be a picture of God," said the girl.

"But," said the father, "No one has ever seen God or knows what God looks like."

"I'm not through yet," said his daughter. "Wait until I'm done."

If You Want To See God --- Wait Until They Have Finished

When you think about things you would like to do, you will likely identify many obstacles that prevent their accomplishment. I don't know why it is, but somehow if you are optimistic, you vastly improve your chances for success. Optimism combined with confidence is so important that if you think you can do it, you probably can. So, if your daughter is drawing a picture of God, be patient, and wait until she is done.

I was attending a relatively dry real estate course and suddenly there developed a very heated discussion about the regulations for multiple agencies.

In the midst of the controversy, one of the students asked whether this material would be on the exam. The teacher responded that it would not. Immediately, all interest in this debate ceased, and we switched to the next topic.

If You Have No Desire Or Need To Know --- Skip To The Next Topic

In connection with knowledge, what is your goal? Are you learning for learning's sake to help yourself for the long term, or are you learning necessary information to help you in the short run? If you are learning for your own knowledge, decide what is important to you and learn it; if you are studying for a test or a meeting, learn what you need to know and, if there is not a need to know, go on to the next topic.

Casey Stengel, the famous New York Yankee baseball manager, was trying out a new center fielder who dropped several fly balls in a row. Casey became disgusted and ran into center field to shag the fly balls himself and mentor his center fielder.

When the first ball was hit to him, he put up his mitt to catch it, but it dropped. Casey threw his mitt to the ground and yelled at the new center fielder, "You got center field so screwed up that nobody can catch a ball now."

When You Are Criticized, Don't Defend Yourself --- Offer The Solution

Yogi Berra, the famous Yankee catcher and manager, said that baseball is 50% physical and 90% mental. He may not have been completely right. However, in business, when the ball is dropped, no matter how or where it is dropped, don't be surprised if you are blamed. And when you are blamed, the best defense is to explain how your team will successfully catch the next ball.

A shiny Mercedes drove by and an 11-year-old girl said, "Boy, when I grow up that's the kind of car I want." Her mother asked what sort of work she was planning to do in order to afford such a car. "I'm going to be a sixth-grade teacher," she replied.

Her mother explained that she might have to set her sights a little higher, as a Mercedes is very expensive.

"Okay," the girl said, "I'll be a seventh-grade teacher."

Guess Again --- If You Want That Mercedes

To be successful in life, you must identify what is really important to you. Once you identify what is really important, it is easier to define your goals. If your goal is to do good, remember that many folks who have a Mercedes never did as much good as either a sixth or seventh-grade teacher.

In the middle of the Depression a multi-millionaire went to two farmers who lived on the outskirts of town, offered them each one million dollars, and asked each of them what they would do with the money.

The first farmer said, "I am going to sell my farm, buy a fishing rod, and enjoy myself."

The second farmer answered, "I am going to keep farming until I lose it all."

Money Isn't Everything --- Some Farmers Don't Want To Go Fishing

Sometimes in business we work with customers or on a project that we intuitively know will not generate a significant result. This is often because we find this aspect of work either highly enjoyable or obligatory. This is fine; but then we should not be disappointed when we don't earn much and don't have much time for fishing.

A couple of out-of-work entertainers were discussing ways to get back onstage. One suggested they work together and proposed, "First, the curtain goes up and then I come out and tell some jokes. Then the curtain comes down. Then the curtain comes up and I dance and sing a few songs. Then...."

At this point he was interrupted by the other who asked, "What am I supposed to do?"

The first guy replied, "The curtain doesn't go up or down by itself."

A Good Teammate Remembers That The Curtain Does Not Go Up By Itself

Being on a team, either as a leader or a member, provides you with a challenge, and that challenge is to contribute toward success. Your participation and your ability to help your team is what will lead you to that success.

This is why it is so important to have a leader with vision, compassion and knowledge and team members who have responsibilities closest to their skills and interests. Sometimes that means telling the jokes, dancing and singing; at other times it means pulling the curtain up and down.

One day, a Schlemiel* was eating a piece of bread that he had buttered, and the bread fell to the ground, butter side up.

The town's people could not believe that the Schlemiel, who never did anything right, could be so lucky as to have the bread fall butter side up.

They went to the rabbi and asked for an explanation. The rabbi studied the Torah and its Commentaries for two days. Then he arose and summoned the town's people. "Do not worry," he said. "The Schlemiel is still the Schlemiel. He buttered the wrong side."

Sometimes You Must Tell Them They Are Right --- Even If They Buttered The Wrong Side

Often, we must support minor decisions even if they are wrong. This minor reinforcement is essential because it allows us to focus on the major goals and changes that we seek to accomplish. I believe that if a company is basically headed in a good direction, it can make many errors along the way and still be successful. For small stuff, forget that they buttered the wrong side. Save your energy for important matters.

---

*Schlemiel" is a Yiddish word for "loser." When a schlemiel fixes things, his tools break; when a schlemiel eats, food ends up on his clothing.

Illustration by Mara Natkin

He buttered the wrong side.

Neil Armstrong, just before he uttered those famous words, "That's one small step for man, one giant leap for mankind," made an unexplained statement, "Good Luck, Mr. Gorsky." For 25 years he refused to explain what that meant. Finally, he explained his comment.

In 1938 when he was a kid in a small Midwestern town, he was playing baseball with a friend in the backyard. His friend hit a fly ball, which landed in the neighbor's yard by the bedroom windows. His neighbors were Mr. and Mrs. Gorsky. As he leaned down to pick up the ball, he heard Mrs. Gorsky shouting at Mr. Gorsky, "Sex! You want Sex! You'll get sex when the kid next door walks on the moon."

Don't Ignore The Impossible --- The Kid Next Door May Walk On The Moon

Often it is only our imagination that prevents us from achieving our goals. So, Good Luck, Mr. Gorsky!

It is now your turn to walk on the moon.
Good luck.

Epilogue

Values, Dreams and Goals

It is quite likely that this will be the final book I write. As I see it, now is my chance to share with you what I think is fun and what is important.

I hope that you agree that, for the most part, the jokes and stories in this book were fun and that identifying values is important. Identifying and working toward your dreams and your goals is important and fun; and succeeding in accomplishing your goals is a lot of fun.

Therefore, at no additional cost, let me share with you some thoughts on Values, Dreams and Goals.

Values: Those qualities which are important to you, which you would like to guide your actions,

Dreams: Your life-long goals which you seek to achieve based upon your Values.

Goals: Those milestones that you would like to achieve within a year and, with sufficient attention, effort and good fortune, you have some reasonable chance to accomplish.

Values

My dad was a gold bug who believed that ending the gold standard and allowing profligate governments to issue fiat money would be the downfall of our personal liberties because economic stability is a major factor that guarantees our personal freedoms. I am sure he was right. But the point of this chapter is to concentrate on intangible values which help us identify those personal qualities that have real value: like respect, integrity and kindness.

I believe that defining our values makes it easier to identify our dreams and accomplish our goals.

My Values

- To act with kindness, patience, graciousness and integrity;

- To be more realistic and practical in my expectations and use of time so that I can better appreciate the moment;

- To foster and maintain good mental and physical health;

- To realize happiness, contentment and satisfaction by being grateful for the blessings which God has bestowed on me and by treating other people with respect and courtesy and receiving similar treatment from them;

- To have a sense of accomplishment by doing things that are meaningful to me while having fun;

- To contribute toward family harmony;

- To continually improve my insight, knowledge and humor; and

- To be practical and charitable with my money, and to pay the Government the least that I am legally obligated to pay.

Dreams

Life is all about choices. Each of us has that unique opportunity to choose our own dreams. Very much like most folks, I dreamed of being happily married and having great kids. Nancy, my wife always tells me that I am happily married and my best friends, whom I can count on to provide me with true counsel, always tell me that my kids, Dan and David are terrific. Therefore, you can see that my most important dreams have already come true.

As Joe E. Lewis said, "You only live once --- but if you work it right, once is enough." The journey to achieve one's dreams is a source of real fulfillment.

My Dreams

Personal:

Considering the time, talent, money, knowledge, confidence and support that I have, here is what I will do:

- Support my family with love and patience.

- Continually maintain good feelings for my extended family.

- Be gracious, warm and friendly with all I meet.

- Focus my energy where my abilities and contributions will be significant.

Business:

- Lead a business that continually improves, has clearly identified focus and values, provides substantial value to its clients --- and is outrageously profitable for its owners and staff.

- Help others to become successful by practicing integrity, concentrating on one thing at a time and working at a relaxed, steady pace.

--- **Goals** ---

"Go To It!
Make the most of every golden minute
It's amazing what determination will do for YOU!
... You CAN do it: GO TO IT!" *

These are the words from the book my dad gave me as a kid.

When I failed, or thought that I failed, I would pick up this little booklet and reread it. It reminded me to try again.

I define a goal as something that I would like to accomplish in a short period of time and certainly no longer than a year.

GOALS FOR THIS YEAR

Personal:
- I will make a list of 5 things to do each day. At day's end, when I review these, I will look back and say, "That was good" or else, I will say, "Shit."

- I will tell myself, "I don't have to do anything today." And I will stop pushing myself to do more than I should.

- I will make each day special with a joke, an event, or a happening, and read at least 30 minutes a day.

- I will make one new friend this year.

- I will take special moments each day to enjoy the beauty of my home and spend quality time with my wife.

- I will keep the positive phone calls long and the negative, irritating ones short.

- I will not become aggravated about any financial matter that is less than (fill in your amount) or wastes less than (fill in your time).

- I will weigh no more than (fill in your goal).

Business:
- I will meet our revenue goal for the year.

- I will think strategically more and short term less.

- I will learn more about (fill in your subject).

---

* *An Executive's Gold Mine of Inspiration* by E. F. G. Gerard, The Executive Company, NY 1964.

Acknowledgements

It is my thought that most people who actually read the acknowledgement page do so because they believe they will be mentioned in it. In order to encourage you to read the full Acknowledgment, I have included several folks who have had nothing to do with it. Examples are Mohammed Ali (boxer), Al Gore (founder of the internet), and Ben Sheets (famous Milwaukee baseball pitcher).

Having worked on this book a great deal, I hope that there are many parts that you liked. Perhaps there were some jokes, stories, or comments that you thought were inappropriate or just poor jokes. Let me point out that I received a great deal of help in writing this book, and so I would caution you against solely blaming me for those portions which you did not like.

It will probably be hard for you to picture how important my wife Nancy is to this book. She not only read each joke and comment multiple times, but also is primarily responsible for the level of its correctness. She transformed this from an amateur effort to its current state by providing the source of illustrations, developing the format, and most importantly, and this is something that you will probably find hard to believe, advising me when my comments were off-base, in poor taste or irrelevant.

My kids, David and Dan, have provided me with sources of great humor throughout their lives and, in addition, have at times increased my need for humor. David and his wife Cheryl did a very thorough job of proof reading and correcting my English and David even graded each of these jokes according to the famous David scale of funniness.

Thanks to my sister-in-law, Eileen Gosman, who contributed her copy editing skills. No piece of bad grammar, poor punctuation or incorrect spelling escaped her careful, professional examination.

The students at Milwaukee Institute of Art and Design, under the guidance of their teacher, Chris Beetow, and MIAD president, Neil Hoffman, did a remarkable job of illustrating this book. They are the type of talented kids that will contribute toward America remaining a country that we are proud of. Their names are: Pacharaporn Bamrungphong, Dana Borremans, Charles Boston, Jonathan Carnehl, Ryan Carter, Janelle Crawford, Audre Delany, Katie Gamb, Kelly Grabko, Eric Hungerford, Risa Marie Johnson, Jia Le Zhang, Abbey Manalli, Abby Marten, Jared Martin, Katie McDonnell, Brittany Miller, Mara Natkin, Rick Peñaloza, Lauren Rubin, Jodi Schomaker, Heidi Schwartz, Rebecca Siahaan, Ashley Webster, Sterling White, Daniel R. Williams, and Alex Wohlrab.

Alex Herrera did a professional job of creating a clean, interesting and consistent format. Thanks, Alex.

Carole Pollack, who illustrated the first edition of this book and has remained my friend through all of my bad jokes, deserves great credit.

I am also indebted to the great comedians Myron Cohen, Milton Berle, Steve Martin, my uncle Jess Marks and my father Ben Einhorn who guided my sense of humor and shared so many jokes with me. Also to those who have told me one or more of these jokes to whom I have not given any credit, please forgive my bad memory. You know who you are and where you are and deserve credit from me which you will never receive.

The talented actors from the Milwaukee Repertory Theater, Torrey Hansen and Lee Ernst, who have assured me that they will bring to life the thoughts in this book will likely deserve special thanks for their future efforts so I mention them now.

And finally, let us not forget the attorneys: you have no idea how much damage they can do!

The End

Quite likely this will be the final book that I write. So allow me to answer the question of how I would like to be remembered...

"He loved his wife Nancy and his family, he was fun to be with, he had a real good sense of right and wrong --- and he wrote a joke book"